THE JOURNAL OF AMAZONIAN LANGUAGES
VOLUME ONE

CONTENTS

Volume 1, Number 2

March 1998

The use of coreferential and reflexive markers in Tupí-Guaraní languages

Cheryl Jensen

Summer Institute of Linguistics

1. Introduction

Tupí-Guaraní is one of the major language families in lowland South America. This family is very diverse geographically, with members all across Brazil, and reaching into French Guiana on the north, Paraguay and Argentina on the south, and Bolivia on the west. The languages of this family have been tentatively divided by Rodrigues (1984/1985) into 8 subgroups, based systematically on their phonological history, but considering other factors as well, as in Table 1:

1 (Guaraní)	Argentina, Bolivia, Brazil, Paraguay	Chiriguano cluster (Ava, Izoceño). Guayaki (Aché). Kaiwá. Mbyá. Nhandéva.
2	Bolivia	Guarayu. Sirionó.
3	Brazil (coastal)	Tupí (extinct). Tupinambá (extinct). Nheengatú. Kokáma.
4	Brazil (GO,MA,MT,-PA)	Avá. Akwawa cluster (Tocantins Asuriní, Suruí of Tocantins, Parakanã). Tapirapé. Tenetehára cluster (Guajajára, Tembé).
5	Brazil (MT,PA)	Xingu Asuriní. Kayabí. Araweté??
6	Brazil (AC,AM, MT,RO)	Apiaká. Kawahíb cluster (Parintintín, Tenharim, and others)
7	Brazil (MT)	Kamaiurá
8	Brazil (AP, MA, PA), French Guiana	South of Amazon: Anambé. Guajá. Urubu-Kaapor. North of Amazon: Emerillon, Wayampi, Zo'é
Abbreviations of Brazilian states: AC Acre; AM Amazonas; AP Amapá; GO Goiás; MA Maranhão; MT Tato Grosso; PA Pará; RO Rondonia		

Table 1: Subgroups of Tupí-Guaraní family

[JAL, vol. 1, no.2, March 1998, pp. 1-49]

1.1 Typological features

Typologically this language family is characterized by head-marking with no dependent-marking to distinguish subjects from objects. The word order in independent clauses is flexible, the most likely basic word order being *SOV or *SVO (Jensen, 1998). There is a split-ergative cross-referencing system in transitive verbs as well as an active/stative distinction in intransitive verbs (see Section 2). A set (Set 1) of prefixes which marks A (subject of transitive verb) and S (subject of intransitive verb) occurs only with independent verbs. Another set of person markers (Set 2) which marks S and O (object of transitive verb) occurs with both independent and dependent verbs. In subordinate clauses the verbs have absolutive cross-referencing and occur in final position. The same set of person markers which cross references S and O is also used to refer to a pronominal genitive on nouns and the object of postpositions. A set of coreferential prefixes (Set 3) occurs in basically the same syntactic contexts as the markers of this set (2), except for independent verbs, when the referent is also the subject of the independent clause (Section 4). There is no indirect discourse in Tupí-Guaraní languages, hence no logophoric reference, nor is there a passive construction.

1.2 Coreferential marking in a nutshell

In English coreferential marking is only explicit and obligatory when a pronominal object, either of the verb (ex. 1) or of a preposition (ex. 2), is identical with the subject.

(1) He killed him. > He killed *himself.*
(2) He bought the car for him. > He bought the car for *himself.*

In this case a special set of pronouns replaces the accusative pronouns. A complete paradigm exists: *myself, ourselves, yourself, yourselves, himself, herself, itself, themselves.*

When a pronominal genitive is identical with the subject, no special form exists, making the referent ambiguous. This is clarified by the optional addition of the word *own:*

(3) He returned to his house. > He returned to *his (own)* house.

The word own may occur with any possessive pronoun: *my (own), our (own), your (own), his (own), her (own), its (own), their (own).*

In Portuguese special forms exist only for third person pronouns, *se* (object of verb) and *si* (argument of the preposition), and are unaltered by gender or number. The existence of forms only for third person is not surprising since only third person presents any potential ambiguity.

(4) Ele o matou. > Ele ***se*** matou.
he him killed he himself killed

(5) a) Ele comprou o carro para ele. >
he bought the car for him

b) Ele comprou o carro para *si* *(mesmo).*
he bought the car for himself (specifically)

However, to emphasize the coreferential relationship in prepositional phrases, regardless of the person or number, it is possible to add the word *mesmo* after the pronoun.

Like English, there is no special form for a coreferential pronominal genitive. But the coreferential relationship can be clarified by the addition of the word *própria*.

(6) a) Ele voltou para *sua* casa. >
he returned to his/her house

b) Ele voltou para *sua (própria)* casa.
he returned to his (own) house

In both languages the trigger for coreferential marking is the subject, and the targets, i.e. the arguments which are recipients of such marking, are pronouns (Wiesemann 1986:442).

In Tupí-Guaraní languages coreferential marking is expressed by a reflexive morpheme **je-* (and its reciprocal counterpart **jo-*) and by a complete set (in various languages and in the protolanguage) of what I refer to as coreferential prefixes: **wi-* *1SG,* **oro-* *'1EX',* **jere-*[1] *1IN',* **e-* *'2SG',* **peje-* *'2PL',* and **o-* *'3'.*

When the direct object is identical with the subject, the reflexive prefix **je-* is combined with the transitive verb stem, resulting in an intransitive verb:

---

[1]Data from languages in subgroups 4 and 7 suggest that the reconstruction should be **jere-* while data from languages in subgroup 5 suggest **jare-*. Rodrigues (personal communication) prefers the latter reconstruction, explaining the forms based on **jere-* as a case of vocalic assimilation, reinforced by analogy with **peje-*. I prefer the reconstruction **jere-*, which occurs in a larger number of languages, and explain the forms based on **jare-* as a case of analogy with **ja-* and **jané*.

(7) *o-i-potár[2] > *o-je-potár
3A-3O-like[3] 3A-REFL-like
'he likes him/her/it' 'he likes himself'

The coreferential object of a postposition is formed by the combination of one of the set of coreferential prefixes, together with the reflexive prefix, and the postposition:

(8) a) *o-i-pycýk i-cupé[4] 'He grasped it for him (other).'
3A-3O-grasp 3-for

b) *o-i-pycýk o-je-upé 'He grasped it for himself.'
3A-3O-grasp 3COR-REFL-for

The coreferential pronominal genitive is expressed by one of the set of coreferential prefixes:

(9) a) *i–čý o-s-epják 'He/she saw his/her mother (someone else's).'
3-mother 3A-3O-see

---

[2]An attempt has been made to follow the conventions used for practical orthographies of Tupí-Guaraní languages in Brazil. In these languages the letter *y* is used to represent the high central unrounded vowel [ɨ] and an apostrophe (') represents the glottal stop. The pronunciation of the phoneme written as *j* ranges from a voiced alveopalatal affricate in the Guaraní languages to a semivowel in Wayampi. Other symbols which appear in this paper are *x* [č] in Tapirapé and Guaraní, *à* [ə] in Guajajára, semivowels *ì* and *ù* in Kayabí, *g* [ŋ] in several languages, *v* [β] in several languages.

[3]Linguistic abbreviations: In relation to word order: SOV Subject, Object, Verb. In relation to referent of person markers: A subject of transitive verb, O object of intransitive verb, S subject of intransitive verb, S_a subject of agentive intransitive verb, S_o subject of nonagentive transitive verb. 1SG first person singular, 1EX first person exclusive, 1IN first person inclusive, 2SG second person singular, 2PL second person plural, 3 third person. 1A+2PL.O portmanteau morpheme referring simultaneously to first person A and second person O. Grammatical morphemes: CAUS causative, CC comitative causative, COMPL completive, COND conditional, COR coreferential, DAT dative, EMPH emphatic, FUT future, FUTIL futility (modal particle), HRSY heresay (evidentiality particle), IMPERS impersonal referent, INTER (interrogative), IRREAL irrealis, LK linking (relational) morpheme, NC nominal case, NEG negative, NOM nominalizer, nonCOR non-coreferential, PUNC punctual, REFL reflexive, SER dependent serial verb, WH when (temporal subordinator), X (in gloss, unspecified A).

[4] Data from some of the more conservative languages, including Tupinambá, suggest the reconstruction of the form **cupé*, whereas others suggest **upé*. Many languages give evidence of the early insertion of a semivowel following the third person prefix: **i-upé* > **i-jupé*. However, I have not encountered data, even from Tupinambá, which suggests that the coreferential form should be **o-je-cupé* rather than **o-je-upé*.

b) *o-čý o-s-epják 'He/she saw his/her own mother.'
3COR-mother 3A-3O-see

In the syntactic contexts where coreferential prefixes occur, they are obligatory, thus reducing the potential for ambiguity in a language family which already has other sources of ambiguity, such as flexibility in word order, which sometimes leaves doubt as to syntactic role when A and O are both third person, and lack of gender. For example, in the following example, **i-čy* can be interpreted as either subject or object, and the **i-* 'third person' gives no indication of gender or number.

(10) *i-čý o-c-epják
3-mother 3A-3O-see

'He/she saw his/her (of another person) mother.' OR
'His/her mother met him/her.'

Like English and Portuguese, the trigger for coreferential marking is the subject. However, the range of targets is more extensive: it is any structure which would normally receive Set 2 person markers (noun, dependent verb, or postposition) where the referent is also coreferential with the subject. In the case of verbs (subordinate or serial) the cross referencing is absolutive, referring to S or O (Dixon 1994:8-9), as in example 11:

(11) a) *o-'ár i-pycýk-VmV 'He fell when (someone) grabbed him[nonCOR].'
3S-fall 3O-grab-WH

b) *o-'ár o-pycýk-VmV 'He fell when (someone) grabbed him [COR].'
3S-fall 3COR-grab-WH

This is an unusual situation grammatically, with the trigger defined on a nominative-accusative basis, at the syntactic level, and the target defined on an ergative-absolutive basis:

TRIGGER	Nominative	A	Ergative	
TRIGGER	Nominative	S	Absolutive	TARGET
	Accusative	O	Absolutive	TARGET

1.3 Versions of coreferential system

As I will show in this paper, some languages have a complete paradigm of coreferential prefixes, even though only the third person referents are potentially ambiguous, and these are used in a wide variety of syntactic contexts. Others have only the third person prefix, which is used in a reduced number of syntactic contexts. In this group of languages, the absolutive cross-referencing system has been largely replaced by the mixed system used with independent verbs (Section 3.1), with a consequent elimination of the context in which the coreferential prefixes originally occurred. Individual Tupí-Guaraní languages fit into one of four possible categories:

Maximal: Complete paradigm of coreferential prefixes; coreferential referencing extended to subordinate clause.

Transitional: Reduction in the number of coreferential prefixes AND/OR coreferential referencing not extended to subordinate clause.

Minimal: Only one coreferential prefix (third person); limited or no oreferential prefixing on verbs other than nominalized forms.

Nonexistent: Complete elimination of coreferential prefixing.

2. Person marker sets

In spite of the widespread geographical distribution there is a large degree of homogeneity within the language family in the area of basic vocabulary and grammatical morphemes, making the morphological reconstruction fairly straightforward for the most part, even though the function of these grammatical morphemes may vary from language to language. This is the case with the four sets of person markers (especially the first two sets) which are an important point of departure for any discussion of Tupí-Guaraní morphosyntax. The reconstructed forms of these person markers for Proto-Tupí-Guaraní (P-T-G) appear in the following table (Jensen, 1990):[5]

	Set 1 **A/S**	**Set 2** **O/S**	**Set 3** **COR O/S**	**Set 4** **portmanteau A+O**
1SG	*a-	*čé[6]	*wi-	
1EX	*oro-	*oré	*oro-	
1IN	*ja-	*jané	*jere-	
2SG	*ere-	*né	*e-	*oro- (1A+2SG.O)
2PL	*pe-	*pé	*peje-	*opo- (1A+2PL.O)
3	*o-	*i-/c-	*o-	

Table 2: Proto-Tupí-Guaraní person marker sets

[5] No reconstruction can be done without the extensive preliminary descriptive field work by many linguists in many languages. Each of these linguists deserves my thanks. The languages on which my reconstruction was based include the following: Subgroup I Chiriguano (also called Bolivian Guaraní), Kaiwá, Old Guaraní, Mbyá Guaraní; Subgroup II Guarayu; Subgroup III Tupinambá; Subgroup IV Assurini do Tocantins (also called Assurini do Trocará), Guajajára, Tapirapé; Subgroup V Kayabí; Subgroup VI Parintintín; Subgroup VII Kamaiurá; and Subgroup VIII Urubu-Kaapor, Wayampi. Reconstruction data can be found in Jensen (1989) and (1998).

[6] The person markers for first and second person in Set 2 are identical with, or reductions of, free pronouns. They are reconstructed as being independent morphemes with independent stress, but in some languages these have become prefixes. The third person prefixes are not derived from pronouns, but occur in complementary distribution with the first and second person markers.

The more conservative languages have a mixed cross-referencing system with independent transitive verbs, using Sets 1, 2, and 4. They have a split-S system for intransitive verbs, using Sets 1 and 2. In all other verb constructions they are cross referenced by an ergative-absolute system, using Set 2 person markers unless the referent (S or O) is coreferential with the subject (S or A) of the main clause. In this case they use Set 3 prefixes. This same system (using Sets 2 and 3) is also used to refer to the pronominal possessor of nouns and the pronominal argument of postpositions.[7] Some of the more innovative languages (those in the minimal category) have eliminated the first and second person markers of Set 3, which is the coreferential set. They have extended the use of prefix Set 1 (A/S) for transitive and agentive intransitive verbs (S_a) so that it occurs in certain syntactic environments which traditionally required O/S marking (Set 2 or 3). In this substitution the **o-* prefix from Set 3 has been reinterpreted as belonging to Set 1. With nouns, postpositions, and nonagentive intransitive verbs (S_o) the Set 2 paradigm has replaced that of Set 3 for first and second persons. In some of the languages in the transitional category, Set 2 rather than Set 1 prefixes have replaced first and second person markers from Set 3.

Besides these four person marker sets, there is a pair of prefixes, **je-* 'reflexive' and **jo-* 'reciprocal'. These have been fused in Guajajára and Wayampi to reflexes of **je-* and in Urubu-Kaapor to the reflex of **jo-*.

In this paper I will provide a syntactic context for the description of coreferential prefixes by describing the non-coreferential prefixes and the environments in which they occur (Section 3). I will also describe the reflexive and reciprocal prefixes, since these also contribute to the overall coreferential system (Section 4). In Section 5 I will give a detailed description of the syntactic environments in which coreferential marking occurs. In these sections (3-5) I will largely use reconstructed forms for Proto-Tupí-Guaraní. Finally I will give a detailed description of the use of coreferential marking according to the categories outlined on the previous page: Maximal (Section 6), Transitional (Section 7), Minimal (Section 8) and Nonexistent (Section 9), using data from representative languages. My conclusions (Section 10) will include the implications for this study in relation to the present tentative subgrouping of languages. Questions for potential further study deal with the origins of the coreferential prefixes and the use of coreferential marking beyond the sentence level for discourse purposes in some languages (Section 11).

---

[7] This system is discussed in detail in Jensen (1990), Jensen (1998), Harrison (1986), and Dixon (1994).

3. The syntactic context of the trigger

The trigger for coreferential marking is the subject (A or S) of the main verb in an independent clause. Thus the trigger is defined on a nominative-accusative basis, even though the overall cross-referencing system in Tupí-Guaraní languages involves various sorts of cross-referencing splits, as will be described in Sections 3 and 5. Whereas it is not unusual cross-linguistically that the trigger should be nominative-accusative, it is probably quite unusual that the verbal constructions which are the recipients, or targets, of coreferential marking follow an ergative-absolutive cross-referencing system.

Depending on the syntactic environment, the main verb in an independent clause may occur as one of two types: independent (Section 3.1) or oblique-topicalized (Section 3.2).

3.1 Independent verbs

Cross referencing on independent verbs is done through split systems: a split-S system in intransitive verbs and a split-ergative system governed by a person hierarchy in transitive verbs. In intransitive verbs, Set 1 (A/S) prefixes occur on more agent-like verbs (ex. 12) and Set 2 (O/S) prefixes occurring on the more object-like ones (ex. 13). As can be seen in example 13, stems are subdivided into two separate classes when they combine with person markers of Set 2. Those of Class 2 require the relational prefix **r-* when the stem is preceded by person markers of first or second person. (Following the second person plural person marker an allomorph **n-* is used.) For third person, this class combines directly with the allomorph **c-*[8], whereas Class 1 stems take the **i-* allomorph. Although the two stems in example 12 are from separate classes, there is no difference in the prefixing from Set 1.

(12) Independent intransitive verbs (S_a)

**a*-có	'I went'	**a*-ikó	'I am (in motion)'
**oro*-có	'we EX went'	**oro*-ikó	'we EX are (in motion)'
**ja*-có	'we IN went'	**ja*-ikó	'we IN are (in motion)'
**ere*-có	'you SG went'	**ere*-ikó	'you SG are (in motion)'
**pe*-có	'you PL went'	**pe*-ikó	'you PL are (in motion)'
**o*-có	'he/she/it/they went'	**o*-ikó	'he/she/it/they is/are (in motion)'

[8] A few Class 2 stems, mostly nouns, take a **t-* prefix instead of **c-*.

(13) Independent intransitive verbs (S_o)

Class 1		*Class 2*	
**čé* katú	'I am good'	**čé r*-orýβ	'I am happy'
**oré* katú	'we EX are good'	**oré r*-orýβ	'we EX are happy'
**jané* katú	'we IN are good'	**jané r*-orýβ	'we IN are happy'
**né* katú	'you SG are good'	**né r*-orýβ	'you SG are happy'
**pé* katú	'you PL are good'	**pé n*-orýβ	'you IN are happy'
**i*-katú	he/she/it/they is/are good'	**c*-orýβ	'he/she/it/they is/are happy'

For transitive verbs there is a direct-inverse system, governed by a person hierarchy (in general terms, 1>2>3). When O is third person, both A and O prefixes occur on the verb: A is marked by the same set used to mark S_a. This prefix, from Set 1, is followed by the third-person O prefix from Set 2 (ex. 14). As in example 13, the class of the stem determines the form of the third person O prefix. In example 14 A is either hierarchically superior to or equal to O. When both are third person, they are not coreferential.

(14) Independent transitive verbs (A - O3)

Class 1		*Class 2*	
**a-i*-potár	`I like[3]'	**a-c*-epják	'I saw [3]'
**oro-i*-potár	'we EX like [3]'	**oro-c*-epják	'we EX saw [3]'
**ja-i*-potár	'we IN like [3]'	**ja-c*-epják	'we IN saw [3]'
**ere-i*-potár	'you SG like [3]'	**ere-c*-epják	`you SG saw [3]'
**pe-i*-potár	'you PL like [3]'	**pe-c*-epják	'you PL saw {3]'
**o-i*-potár	'[3] like(s) [3]'	**o-c*-epják	'[3] saw [3]'

The object prefixes occur regardless of whether a free nominal object is present in the clause, as in the following examples from Tupinambá (ex. 15):

(15) kunumĩ <u>a-i-</u>nupã 'I beat the boy.'
<u>a-i-</u>nupã kunumĩ 'I beat the boy.'

An object may also be incorporated in the verb. In this situation the verb is detransitivized, provided the object is not possessible, and the object prefix does not occur, as in Tupinambá:

(16) a-kunumĩ-nupã 'I boy-beat.'

When A is hierarchically inferior to O, only O is marked on the verb, using Set 2 prefixes (example 17). This is an indirect system. In this case the A, which is not expressed morphologically by verbal cross referencing, may be either third or second person, but not first person. Once again, the stems from Class 2 require the relational prefix *r*-.

(17) Independent transitive verbs (O>A)

Class 1		*Class 2*	
**čé* potár	'(2) or (3) likes me'	**čé r*-epják	'(2) or (3) saw me'
**oré* potár	'(2) or (3) likes us EX'	**oré r*-epják	'(2) or (3) saw us EX'
**jané* potár	'(3) likes us IN'	**jané r*-epják	'(3) saw us IN'
**né* potár	'(3) likes you SG'	**né r*-epják	'(3) saw you SG'
**pé* potár	'(3) likes you PL'	**pé n*-epják	'(3) saw you PL'

Note that the O is never third person, since it must be hierarchically superior to A. In the following examples from Tupinambá, the third person A is expressed by a free noun preceding or following the verb, as in examples 18-19, and the hierarchically superior O is expressed on the verb.

(18) kunumĩ <u>né</u> r-epják 'The boy saw you..'
<u>né</u> r-epják kunumĩ 'The boy saw you..'

(19) <u>sjé</u> nupã sjé r-uβ-a 'My father beat me.'
sjé r-uβ-a <u>sjé</u> nupã 'My father beat me.'

When A is second person this is indicated by a separate word: **jepe* '2SG' or **pejepe* '2PL', as in the following example from Tupinambá.[9]

(20) (ndé) sjé r-epják jepé 'You saw me.'
(2SG) 1SG LK-see- 2SG.A

When both A and O are speech-act participants, and A is hierarchically superior to O (i.e. 1st person A and 2nd person O), Set 4 prefixes are used to indicate A and O jointly (example 21). Like the prefixes from Set 1, these prefixes are not affected by stem class.

(21) Independent transitive verbs (A1 + O2)

Class 1		*Class 2*	
**oro*-potár	'I/we like you SG'	**oro*-epják	'I/we saw you SG'
**opo*-potár	'I/we like you PL'	**opo*-epják	'I/we saw you PL'

In sum, the system used with independent transitive verbs, as reconstructed for Proto-Tupí-Guaraní, may be described as a combination direct (example 14), inverse (example 17), and portmanteau (example 21) systems. Set1 and Set 4 prefixes are used only in this context.

---

[9]When A is second person and O is first person, many languages indicate the A through a separate word derived from the protoforms **jepe* '2SG.A' or **pejepe* '2PL.A' rather than the normal free pronouns **ené* and **pe...ẽ*, respectively. A similarity to the coreferential (Set 3) prefixes **e-* and **peje-* suggests a possible path of derivation. In this case, it would seem more accurate to describe them as forms coreferential with A rather than forms directly indicating A itself.

This system is used by the majority of Tupí-Guaraní languages in independent verbs, that is, in the main verb of independent clauses. Phonologically the main variation is that *č and *c have weakened in various languages, resulting in *s, h,* or *0,* which are merged in all but subgroup 1. Morphologically the main variation is that in a number of languages (subgroups 4-8) the third person O prefix (**i-* or **c-*) does not co-occur with the prefixes of Set 1 in transitive verbs, resulting in forms like *a-potar* instead of **a-i-potár*. Besides this, there is variation in the form of the Set 4 prefix **opo-* (Jensen 1987).

Even when A is not cross referenced on a transitive verb, it still acts as the trigger for coreferential marking.

3.2 Oblique-topicalized verbs

When an oblique (adverb, postpositional phrase, or temporal subordinate clause) is fronted to the initial position of an independent clause for discourse purposes, the main verb occurs in the oblique-topicalized (OBTOP) form (Harrison 1986:417). This verb requires ergative-absolutive cross-referencing, and occurs with an OBTOP suffix. In some languages (Guajajára and Kamaiurá) this construction occurs only when the subject is third person, in others (Tupinambá (ex. 22-24), Xingu Asuriní, and Kayabí), when the subject is either first or third. When the subject is second person (or possibly first person), only the independent verb form occurs. When S or O in the form of a noun directly precedes the verb, no person markers need occur on the verb, as in example 24.

(22) kwesé **i-só-w**
yesterday 3-go-OBTOP
'Yesterday he went.'

(23) kwesé pajé sjé **subán-i**
yesterday shaman 1SG suck-OBTOP
'Yesterday the shaman treated me (by sucking).'

(24) kó pajé r-ekó-w
here shaman LK-be-OBTOP
'Here is the shaman.'

4. Reflexive and reciprocal prefixing

4.1 On verbs

When the object of a transitive verb is coreferential with the subject, a reflexive prefix **je-* (ex. 26) is used. This prefix occurs in the same position as, and therefore contrasts with, the use of the third person object prefix (ex. 25). It is a valence-changing prefix, detransitivizing a TV and making the A and its coreferential O into a S.[10] Consequently in independent verbs it occurs only with prefixes of Set 1.

(25) * a-*i*-potár 'I like [3]' **Third person object**

(26) * a-*je*-potár 'I like myself' **Reflexive**
* oro-*je*-potár 'we EX like ourselves
* ja-*je*-potár 'we IN like ourselves'
* ere-*je*-potár 'you SG like yourself'
* pe-*je*-potár 'you PL like yourselves'
* o-*je*-potár '[3] like(s) [3]self/selves'

Actions performed on one's own body parts require the reflexive marker when the object is incorporated into the verb construction, as in the following example from Wayampi:[11]

(27) a-ji-po-kusu
1SG-REFL-hand-wash
'I washed my hands.'

Without the reflexive the incorporated possessible object is interpreted as belonging to someone else, as in example 28. In this case the possessor is raised to the position of direct object and the verb remains transitive, in contrast to the example 16, where the incorporated noun is nonpossessible.

(28) a-po-kusu[12]
1SG-hand-wash
'I washed his/her hands.'

Parallel to the reflexive prefix is a reciprocal prefix **jo*-, which of necessity combines only with plural person markers, as in example 29.

(29) * oro-*jo*-potár 'we EX like each other' **Reciprocal**
* ja-*jo*-potár 'we IN like each other'
* pe-*jo*-potár 'you PL like each other'
* o-*jo*-potár '[3] like each other'

It appears that all Tupí-Guaraní languages retain the use of a reflexive prefix for coreferential objects. Therefore no further discussion will be made of

[10]Sometimes the reflexive prefix is used to deemphasize the subject. Hence, the verb **a-je-mo'e* has two possible translations: 'I learned, I taught myself'.

[11]Object incorporation only reduces the valency of the verb when the object is not possessible. When the object is possessible, the possessor becomes the direct object.

[12]In PTG this might have the third person prefix **i*- following the subject prefix **a*-.

them in this paper, except to mention that three Tupí-Guaraní languages have eliminated the **je-/jo-* contrast. In Guajajára and Wayampi the reflex of **je-* is retained, and with a plural subject it can mean either reflexive or reciprocal. In Urubu-Kaapor the reflex of **jo-* is retained. In example 30, the form in the three languages has the two possible interpretations.

(30)	oro-*ji*-pota (WA)	'we EX like ourselves'	**Reflexive**
	uru-*ze*-putar (Gj)	'we EX like each other'	**Reciprocal**
	uru-*ju*-putar (Ur)		

4.2 On postpositions

The reflexive and reciprocal prefixes also occur in postpositional phrases, in combination with coreferential prefixes, when the argument of the phrase is coreferential with the subject, as in example 31. This is discussed in further detail in Section 5.4.

(31) *o-je-pypé 'inside himself'

In sum, the reflexive and reciprocal prefixes occur in the following constructions:

- Verbs when the O is coreferential with the subject.
- Verbs when the possessor of an incorporated object is coreferential with the subject.
- Postpositions, in combination with coreferential prefixes, when the argument is coreferential with the subject.

5. The target constructions for coreferential prefixing

In Proto-Tupí-Guaraní and in the conservative languages of the family the cross referencing on all dependent verb forms (subordinate verb, serial verb, or nominalization) is absolutive (referring to S in intransitive verbs and O in transitive verbs). This cross referencing is done by the person markers of Set 2, provided the referent is not coreferential with the subject (A or S) of the main verb. There is no split-S contrast in this context nor is the person **oré* hierarchy in operation, as can be seen in examples 32- 34.

(32) Dependent intransitive verbs (S_a)

Class I		*Class II*	
* *čé* có	'I go'	* *čé* r-ekó	'I am (in motion)'
	'we EX go happy'	**oré* r-ekó	'we EX are'
* *jané* có	'we IN go'	**jané* r-ekó	'we IN are'
* *né* có	'you SG go'	**né* r-ekó	'you SG are'
* *pé* có	'you PL go'	**pé* n-ekó	'you PL are'
* *i*-có	'[3] goes'	**c*-ekó	'[3] is/are'

(33) Dependent intransitive verbs (S_o)

Class I		*Class II*	
* *čé* katú	'I am good'	**čé* r-orýβ	'I am happy'
* *oré* katú	'we EX are good'	**oré* r-orýβ	'we EX are happy'
* *jané* katú	'we IN are good'	**jané* r-orýβ	'we IN are happy'
* *né* katú	'you SG are good'	**né* r-orýβ	'you SG are happy'
* *pé* katú	'you PL are good'	**pé* n-orýβ	'you PL are happy'
* *i*-katú	'[3] is/are good'	**c*-orýβ	'[3] is/are happy'

(34) Dependent transitive verbs (O)

Class I		*Class II*	
**čé* potár	'X likes me'	* *čé* r-epják	'X sees me'
* *oré* potár	'X likes us EX'	**oré* r-epják	'X sees us EX'
* *jané* potár	'X likes us IN'	**jané* r-epják	'X sees us IN'
* *né* potár	'X likes you SG'	**né* r-epják	'X sees you G'
* *pé* potár	'X likes you PL'	**pé* n-epják	'X sees you PL'
* *i*-potár	'X likes [3]'	**c*-epják	'X sees [3]'

The possessor on nouns and the argument of a postposition are also referenced by Set 2 markers. If the referent of the dependent verb, noun, or postposition is coreferential with A or S, a coreferential prefix from Set 3 is used instead of the normal Set 2 markers, as in example 35.

(35)	* *wi*-có	'I went [COR]'
	* *oro*-có	'we EX went [COR]'
	* *jere-có*	'we INwent [COR]'
	* *e*-có	'you SG went [COR]'
	* *peje*-có	'you PL went [COR]'
	* *o*-có	'[3] went [COR]'

The *r*- morpheme does not occur in this context with Class II stems.

However, with certain stems a *t-* occurs between **wi-* and the stem, as in example 36.

(36) **wi*-t-ekó 'I am (in motion) [COR]'

The following sections describe the normal and the coreferential marking of subordinate verbs (4.1), dependent serial verbs (4.2), nouns (4.3), and postpositions (4.4).

5.1 Subordinate verbs

Subordinate clauses, indicated by brackets in the examples, are used in Tupí-Guaraní languages to indicate information of a temporal nature (simultaneous or sequential). In this type of construction the verb occurs in final position, suffixed by a temporal subordinate marker **-(r)VmV*[13] 'simultaneous/conditional' or **-(r)ire* 'sequential'. Subordinate clauses most frequently occur preposed in relation to the independent clause, although data from some languages show them in a postposed position as well. If they are preposed, the verb from the independent clause must take the oblique-topicalized form if its subject is third (and possibly first) person, as in the following examples from Tocantins Asuriní.

(37) [se-nopo-ramo] ere-poka 'When X beat me, you laughed.'
1SG-beat-WH 2SG-laugh

(38) [se-ha-ramo] i-ha-potar-i se-r-opi
1SG-go-WH 3-go-FUT-OBTOP 1SG-LK-with
'When I go, he will go with me.'

5.1.2 Normal cross referencing on subordinate verbs

The verb is normally cross-referenced by a person marker from Set 2 (ex. 39) or by a noun immediately preceding the verb stem (ex. 40).

(39)	**čé* có-rVmV	'if/when I go'	S_a
	**čé* katú-rVmV	'if/when I am good'	S_o
	**čé* r-epják-VmV	'if/when X sees me'	O
(40)	**kunumĩ* có-rVmV[14]	'if/when the boy goes'	S_a
	**kunumĩ* katú-rVmV	'if/when the boy is good'	S_o
	**kunumĩ* r-epják-VmV	'if/when X sees the boy'	O

[13] The vowels in the morpheme marking subordinate clauses cannot be reconstructed. Some languages have forms like *ramo* while others have forms like *reme*.

[14] The vowels in the morpheme marking subordinate clauses cannot be reconstructed. Some languages have forms like *ramo* while others have forms like *reme*.

5.1.3 Coreferential marking on subordinate verbs

Coreferential marking on subordinate verbs, as I am reconstructing it for Proto-Tupí-Guaraní, involves a complete paradigm, including all the forms listed in example 35 (and in Set 3 of Table 2). This represents the pattern which I describe for Maximal use languages (Section 6); there are other languages which use only the third person prefix in this context.

In the pairs of examples in (41-42), the subordinate verb is agentive intransitive. When the subject of the independent verb is first or third person I am putting it in the OBTOP form because of the preposed subordinate clause.[15] In the sentences marked a), the S_a the subordinate verb is not coreferential with the subject of the main clause. Therefore the normal Set 2 person markers are used. In the examples marked b), the S of the subordinate verb is coreferential with the subject of the main verb. Therefore the subordinate verb receives coreferential prefixes. The same is true for examples (43-44), in which the subordinate verb is nonagentive intransitive.

(41) a) *[*čé* có-rVmV] i-'ár-i 'when I came [nonCOR] he fell'

b) *[*wi*-có-rVmV] čé 'ár-i 'when I went [COR] I fell'

(42) a) * [*né* có-rVmV] i-'ár-i 'when you SG went [nonCOR] he fell'

b) *[*e*-có-rVmV] ere-'ár 'when you went [COR] you SG fell'

(43) a) *[*i*-katú-rVmV] c-orýβ-i 'when he [nonCOR] is good he is happy'

b) *[*o*-katú-rVmV] c-orýβ-i 'when he [COR] is good he is happy'

(44) a) *[*jané* katú-rVmV] c-orýβ-i' when we IN are good [nonCOR] he is happy'

b) *[*jere*-katú-rVmV] jané r-orýβ-i 'when we IN are good [COR] we IN are happy'

In the pairs of examples in (45-46), the subordinate verb is transitive. Therefore it cross references O. In the sentences marked a), the O of the subordinate verb is not coreferential with the subject of the independent clause. Therefore no coreferential prefix is used. In the sentences marked b), the O of the subordinate verb is coreferential with the subject of the independent clause and therefore receives a coreferential prefix.

(45)a) *[*oré* pycýk-VmV] i-'ár-i 'when he grabbed us EX [nonCOR] he fell'

b) *[*oro*-pycýk-VmV] oré 'ár-i 'when he grabbed us EX [COR] we fell'

---

[15] In some languages the subordinate clauses are predominantly preposed as in exs. 41-44. Ex. 11 is comparable to exs. 45-46 except that the subordinate is shown in postposed position.

(46) a) *[*pé* pycýk-VmV] i-'ár-i 'when he grabbed you PL[nonCOR] he fell'

b)*[*peje*-pycýk-VmV] pe-'ár 'when he grabbed you PL [COR] you PL fell'

Some languages, such as Old Guaraní (D. Rodrigues 1997) and Tocantins Asuriní (Nicholson 1978), have a restriction which disallows the use of subordinate clauses when the S or A is coreferential with the S or A of the independent clauses. In these causes there is a split between subordinate verbs for non-coreferential subjects and dependent serial verbs (next section) for coreferential subjects. However, there are many languages which do not have this restriction for subordinate clauses.

5.2 Serial verb constructions

In Tupí-Guaraní languages an action or a series of actions having the same subject may be perceived as part of a single event and expressed as a series overbs in a single clause. The initiating verb (indicated by underlining in the examples) in the series takes the independent (ex. 47, from Tupinambá) or oblique-topicalized (ex. 48, from Tupinambá) form and is cross referenced accordingly (i.e., by the same system as described in Section 2.1 or 2.2). This verb is followed by what in most languages of the family is a dependent verb (italicized),[16] which receives absolutive cross-referencing. I am referring to thisas a serial verb construction, in spite of the dependency marking on the non-initiating verb.[17]

(47) o-úr kunumĩ *r-epják-a*
3-come boy LK-see-SER
'He came to see the boy.'

(48) kó sjé anám-a r-úr-i pá né r-apé pe
here 1SG relative-NC LK-come-OBTOP all 2SG LK-path to

né r-epják-a
2SG LK-see-SER
'All my relatives came here to your path, to see you.'

[16] This verb receives a suffix which has various allomorphs: *-a* following a C, **-aβo* following a V, and **-ta* following the semivowel **j*. These allomorphs are subject to further morphophonemic rules, including nasalization of the consonant in **-ta* and **-aβo*, and absorption of the initial vowel in the form **-aβo*.

[17] What I am referring to as a serial verb construction has the following properties of a single predicate: the verbs refer to aspects of a single event, they have shared tense/aspect markings, they have a single subject, and sometimes they have a shared object as well. However, in the proto-language and many, but not all, of the dependent languages, there is a suffix showing dependency on all but the initial verb. The verb with the dependency suffix is referred to by Rodrigues in Portuguese as a *gerúndio*; in English this would be more accurately called a participle. Dooley (1991) refers to the construction as a "double verb construction."

In some languages, such as Tocantins Asuriní, certain verbs, such as those which mean 'come' and 'to be (in motion)', have become grammaticalized to convey aspectual information, such as direction and continuous action, and developed into a distinct set of auxiliary verbs. In some languages, such as Wayampi, the dependency marking has been eliminated in all of the formerly dependent serial verbs.

5.2.1 Transitive dependent serial verbs

The initiating verb may be either intransitive (as in the examples above) or transitive (examples 49-50). The shared subject is marked on the independent serial verb as permitted by cross-referencing rules. In example 48, where the initiating verb takes the oblique-topicalized form, S is referred to only by a noun directly preceding the verb. In example 50, O rather than A is cross-referenced on the independent verb because of the hierarchy rule. The shared subject is not cross-referenced on either of the verbs, neither on the initiating verb because of the person hierarchy nor on the dependent transitive verb because of the absolutive cross-referencing.

(49) *<u>a-i-nupã</u> *i-juká-βo*
1SG-3-beat 3-kill-SER
'I beat it and killed it.'

(50) *<u>čé pycýk</u> *čé nupã-mo*
1SG grab 1SG beat-SER
'(Someone) grabbed me and beat me.'

Some languages (Tupinambá and Mbyá Guaraní) allow the portmanteau prefixes (example 21) to occur with the dependent transitive verb.

5.2.2 Coreferential marking on intransitive dependent serial verbs

When the dependent serial verb is intransitive, the coreferential subject is referenced, using the special set of coreferential makers. A complete paradigm follows in example 51. The independent verb form of 'I sleep' is **a-kér,* whereas the dependent serial verb form is **wi-kér-a*.

(51)	*a-có	*wi*-kér-a	'I went and slept'
	*oro-có	*oro*-kér-a	'we EX went and slept'
	*ja-có	*jere*-kér-a	'we IN went and slept'
	*ere-có	*e*-kér-a	'you SG went and slept'
	*pe-có	*peje*-kér-a	'you PL went and slept'
	*o-có	*o*-kér-a	'[3] went and slept'

Non-agentive intransitive serial verbs also receive the coreferential markers, but a different suffix *(-ramo/-amo)* is used to indicate the serial verb construction, as in *wi-katú-ramo* 'I being good' or 'in order for me to be good'.

5.3 Nouns

5.3.1 Simple nouns

On simple nouns, the Set 2 morphemes are used to indicate a pronominal possessor. This genitive may indicate possession (ex. 52,54), kinship (ex. 53),or whole-part relationships (ex. 55).

(52)	*Class I*		(53)	*Class II*	
	**čé* kyčé	'my knife'		**čé* r-úβ	'my father'
	**oré* kyčé	'our EX knife'		**oré* r-úβ	'our EX father'
	**jané* kyčé	'our IN knife'		**jané* r-úβ	'our IN father'
	**né* kyčé	'your SG knife'		**né* r-úβ	'your SG father'
	**pé* kyčé	'your PL knife'		**pé* n-úβ	'your PL father'
	**i*-kyčé	'[3]'s knife'		**t*-úβ[18]	'[3]'s father'

In examples 54-55 a nominal genitive precedes a possessed noun. The genitive, in turn, has a possessive prefix from Set 2. The possessed noun **kyčé* 'knife' is from Class I. The nouns **ú*/ 'father' and **ecá* 'eye' are from Class II and therefore have an **r*- prefix between themselves and the genitive.

(54) *t-úβ-a[19] kyčé 'his father's knife'
(55) *t-úβ-a r-ecá 'his father's eye'

5.3.2 Coreferential marking on nouns

When the possessor of a noun is coreferential with the subject of the main verb, it is marked with a coreferential prefix. In example 56 a), the possessor (1SG) is not coreferential with the subject (3SG) and therefore it receives a normal Set 2 person marker. In b) the possessor (1SG) is coreferential with the subject and therefore receives a coreferential prefix. Even if the object, rather than the subject, is cross referenced on the verb, the rule for coreferentiality still depends on the subject. Thus in c) even though the cross-referencing on both the verb and the noun refer to the same person, no coreferential prefixing is used, since the verb cross-references O not A. Conversely, we can say that

---

[18] This morpheme is from subclass IIb, which has **t*- instead of **c*- as a third person prefix.

[19] When a consonant-final nouns occurs syntactically as a noun (i.e. as a subject, object, genitive, or object of a postposition, it receives a 'nominal case' suffix **-a*. Vowel-final nouns occur with a zero suffix.

the object is coreferential, not with A but with the possessor of A, and therefore does not receive coreferential marking.

(56) a) **čé* cý o-c-epják 'he saw my mother' OR 'my mother saw him'

b) **wi*-cý a-c-epják 'I saw my mother'

c) **čé* cý *če r*-epják 'my mother saw me'

5.3.3 Nominalizations

There are three types of nominalizations which are formed by the addition of a suffix to the verb stems: *-*a* 'nominalizer indicating action (or state, in the case of descriptive verbs)[20], *-*áβ* 'nominalizer indicating circumstance (time, place, or instrument)', and *-*ár* ' 'nominalizer indicating agent'.[21] Like simple nouns, these nominalizations combine with person markers from Set 2. However, in the case of these nominalizations, the genitive construction refers to the absolutive referent of the verb. Example 57 show the nominalization of action or state, combining with person markers from Set 2, which refer to S_o, S_a, and O, respectively.

(57) **i*-katú-í 'his (state of) being good'
**i*-có-í 'his (action of) going'
**i*-potár-a 'the action of liking him (O)'

The following examples show the use of Set 2 person markers with the nominalizations of circumstance (ex. 58-59) and agent (ex. 60), once again referring to S (ex. 58) or O (ex. 59-60).

(58) **čé* có-cáβ 'the circumstances (time or place) of my going'

(59) **čé* r-epják-áβ 'the circumstances (time or place) of my being seen, or of (someone) seeing me'

(60) **né* r-epják-ár 'the person that sees you (SG); your see-er'

Another nominalizing morpheme, which occurs only with transitive verbs, is *emi*- 'nominalizer indicating object'. This nominalization may also combine

---

[20] The *-*a* morpheme can be looked upon as the combination of a verb with the 'nominal case' suffix. It occurs with consonant-final stems, and a zero suffix occurs with vowel-final stems.

[21] In many Tupí-Guaraní languages the form derived from *-*áβ* nominalizes both action and circumstance. In the case of the *-*áβ* and *-*ár* morphemes, *-*cáβ* and *-*cár* allomorphs occur with vowel-final stems and *-*taβ* and *-*tár* allomorphs occur with diphthong-final stems, the semivowel of the diphthong being a palatal.

with the person markers from Set 2. The nominalizer is a Class II morpheme, requiring the **r*- prefix. In this case the genitive refers to the agent (A) of the action, as shown in example 61.

(61) **jané r-emi*-potár 'who/what we IN like'

The *emi*- morpheme is unique in being the only nominalizing prefix. This structure is also unique in that the referent of the Set 2 morpheme with which it combines refers to A.[22]

As I have demonstrated, the same set of prefixes may refer to A, O, or S, depending on the type of nominalization and the verb stem with which it combines. Since the coreferential prefixes replace the prefixes of Set 2, it is particularly important to be aware of the grammatical referent of these person markers in nominalizations.

In terms of coreferential prefixing, nominalizations are treated like other nouns. But it is important to remember that in the nominalization of a transitive verb, the "possessive" prefix refers to the object and not the subject, with the exception of the *emi*- construction. In example 62 a), the teacher may be either A or O. If he is A, it is ambiguous whose teacher he is. If he is O, he taught someone else other than the A, so no coreferential prefix is used. In b) the teacher is O, and is specifically the teacher of A. Therefore a coreferential prefix is used. Likewise in 63 a) the student may be A or O, but if he is O he is not the student of A. In b) he is O and is the student of A, as indicated by the coreferential marking.

(62)	a) **i*-mo'é-cár-a o-i-potár	'his teacher likes him' OR 'he likes his [nonCOR] teacher'
	b) **o*-mo'é-cár-a o-i-potár	'he likes his [COR] teacher'
(63)	a) **c*-emi-mo'é o-i-potár	'his student likes him' OR 'he likes his [nonCOR] student'
	b) **o*-emi-mo'é o-i-potár	'he likes his [COR] student'

5.4 Postpositions

5.4.1 Normal inflection of postpositions

When postpositions have a pronominal argument, this is indicated by a prefix from Set 2.

---

[22] An alternative analysis of this structure is that the *emi*- morpheme somehow decreases the transitivity of the verb, parallel to such morphemes as the reflexive and reciprocal prefixes (Section 3.0), so that the referent of the genitive construction becomes S (Jensen 1990:128).

(64)

Class I		*Class II*	
* *čé* cupé	'to/for me'	* *čé* r-upí	'with (led by) me'
* *oré* cupé	'to/for us EX'	* *oré* r-upí	'with (led by) us EX'
* *jané* cupé	'to/for us IN'	* *jané* r-upí	'with (led by) us IN'
* *né* cupé	'to/for you SG'	* *né* r-upí	'with (led by) you SG'
* *pé* cupé	'to/for you PL'	* *pé* n-upí	'with (led by) you PL'
* *i*-cupé	'to/for [3]'	* *c*-upí	'with (led by) [3]'

5.4.2 Coreferential marking on postpositions

Coreferential prefixes are used with postpositions when the object of the postposition is also the subject of the sentence. In this construction the

reflexive *je-* or reciprocal *jo-* is inserted between the coreferential prefix and the stem. In example 65 a) the object of the postposition has a different referent than the subject, although both are third person. Therefore the marking on the postposition is not coreferential. In b) as well, the object of the postposition (1SG) is not coreferential with the subject . In c) the object of the postposition is coreferential with the subject and therefore receives the coreferential prefix together with the reflexive prefix.

(65) a) *kyčé o-i-pycýk *i*-cupé 'he grasped a knife for him [nonCOR]'

b) *kyčé o-i-pycýk *čé* cupé 'he grasped a knife for me'

c) *kyčé a-i-pycýk *wi-je*-upé 'I grasped a knife for myself [COR]'

If the sentence has a plural interpretation, the reflexive *je-* prefix in 66 a) indicates that each subject is performing the action for himself. In b) the action is reciprocal, as indicated by the prefix *jo-*, but since the subjects are members of the same group as the objects of the postposition, the coreferential prefix still occurs on the postposition together with the reciprocal prefix.

(66) a) *o-i-pycýk *o-je*-upé ' he/they grasped it for himself/themselves'

b) *o-i-pycýk *o-jo*-upé 'they grasped it for each other'

In sum, the coreferential prefixes occur in the following constructions:

- Subordinate verbs whose cross-referencing (O, S_a or S_o) is coreferential with the subject (A or S) of the main clause (Section 5.1).
- Dependent serial intransitive (S_a or S_o) verbs since S, which is cross referenced on it, is coreferential with the subject (A or S) of the main verb (Section 5.2).
- Nouns whose possessor is coreferential with the subject (A or S) of the main verb of the clause to which it pertains (Section 5.3).

- Nominalizations, like other nouns, when the possessor (O, S_a or S_o of the verb stem when the verb is nominalized by a suffix; A when the transi tive verb is nominalized by *emi-*) is coreferential with the subject (A or S) of the main verb of the clause to which it pertains (Section 5.3).
- Postpositions whose argument is coreferential with the subject (A or S) of the main verb of the clause to which it pertains. In this context the coreferential prefix occurs together with the reflexive or reciprocal prefix (Section 5.4)

6. Maximal version of coreferential system

Several languages of the Tupí-Guaraní language family use coreferential markers in a way approximating the reconstructed system that I have just described. In some cases there is no direct contradiction of the system, but one of the syntactic structures for which I have reconstructed its operation does not occur, as in Tocantins Asuriní. In other cases the syntactic structures occur but one of the coreferential morphemes on superficial inspection does not appear to be related to the protoform, as in Kayabí and Xingu Asuriní. There is a complete set of coreferential prefixes and these occur in various syntactic constructions: on nouns, postpositions, and verbs when the referent is coreferential with the subject. These languages also retain the traditional cross-referencing on verbs (active/stative system and person hierarchy in independent verbs, with absolutive cross-referencing on the various types of dependent verbs).

6.1 Tocantins Asuriní

In Tocantins Asuriní (a member of the Akwawa[23] cluster of subgroup 4) the full set of coreferential prefixes occurs:

we-, oro-, sere-, e-, pese-, o-/w-

These prefixes occur with transitive subordinate verbs, intransitive serial verbs, nouns, and postpositions. In subordinate clauses, when the O of a transitive verb is identical with the subject of the main verb, the coreferential prefix is used, as in example 67.

(67) [*we*-nopo -ramo] a-ha-pota (ise)
1SG.COR-beat-if 1SG-go-FUT 1SG
'If (someone) beats me, I will go away.'

However, there is no comparable construction for intransitive verbs. This

[23] According to Auristeia Souza e Silva (Parakanã) the coreferential system is comparable to that in Asurini, though no study has been made beyond the level of the sentence. Data collected by Albert Graham show a full set of coreferential markers in Suruí as well.

would require that the subject of the subordinate clause be coreferential with the subject of the independent clause. According to Nicholson (1978:59), when the subject of the independent clause is the same as that of the dependent clause, the verb of the dependent clause takes the form of a serial verb and does NOT have the suffix *-ramo*. It still retains the coreferential prefixing, as in example 68:

(68) [*we*-to-ta] a-'o.
1SG.COR-come-SER 1SG-eat
'After I came, I ate.'

In other words, the coreferential prefixing exists, but the subordinate structure itself doesn't.

The coreferential system is intact for serial verbs, as in example 69:

(69) ere-ha *e*-seegat-a[24]
2SG-go 2SG.COR-sing-SER
'You (SG) went singing.'

In this language a set of auxiliary verbs has been derived from dependent intransitive serial verbs. These verbs occur without the serial verb suffix but retain the coreferential prefixing, as in example 70:

(70) mo'yra a-apo we-ka 'I am making beads.'
A-ata we-ha ka'a pe 'I went hunting in the jungle .'
(Lit. 'I hunted, going, in the jungle')

Nouns receive coreferential prefixes when their possessor is coreferential with the subject. Compare the non-coreferential prefix in 71 a) with the coreferential in b).

(71) a) ere-ha-pota *s*-aga pype 'You will go to his house.'
2SG-go-FUT 3-house to
b) a-ha-pota *w*-aga[25] pype 'He will go to his own house.'

These prefixes occur for other persons as well, as in example 72.

(72) *we*-tyroa a-kotog 'I sew my own clothes.'

Nominalizations, like other nouns, receive coreferential prefixes. In example 73 the coreferential prefix is the S argument of the nominalized verb.

---

[24] According to Harrison (p.c.) the *t* is a case of devoicing (<**r*) in the combination with the serial verb suffix.

[25] In this language the third person coreferential prefix has an allomorph *w*- which occurs when the stem begins with *e* or *a*. In this language vowel shift occurred, as seen in such forms as *ha* 'go' *(<*có)*.

(73) a-ha (ise) *we*-ke-hawa pype
1SG-go 1SG 1SG.COR-sleep-NOM to
'I went to my sleeping place.'

Postpositions also receive coreferential prefixes, as in example 74. In a) this prefix co-occurs with the reciprocal prefix, and in b) with the reciprocal prefix.

(74) a) a-se'eg *we*-se-ope 'I sang to myself.'

b) sa-se'eg *sere*-so-ope 'We (IN) sang to each other.'

6.2 Tapirapé

The full set of coreferential prefixes also occurs in Tapirapé (another member of subgroup 4), as can be seen in the following examples cited by Leite (1987):

we-, ara-, xere-, e-, pexe-, a-/w-

When the O of the subordinate clause is coreferential with the subject of the independent clause, the coreferential prefix is used, as in example 75.

(75) [*we*-xokã-ramõ] ã-xay'a
1SG.COR-beat-COND 1SG-cry
'If (someone) beats me , I'll cry.'

Leite gives no examples of subordinate intransitive coreferential verbs, which would suggest that in this language, as in Tocantins Asuriní, a shift of syntactic structures took place.

Coreferential prefixes occur in serial intransitive verbs, both agentive and non-agentive, as in examples 76 a) and b), respectively.

(76) a) ã-xaok ekwe *we*-yytãp-a
1SG-bathe ? 1SG.COR-swim-SER
'I'll bathe and afterwards I'll swim.'

b) xe-kane'o *we*-ty'ã-ramõ
1SG-tired 1SG.COR-hungry-SER
'I'm tired and hungry.'

Coreferential prefixes also indicate the genitive on nouns, as in examples 77-78.

(77) xe-ropy *a*-'yãra a-ma-xerep
1SG-father 3COR-canoe 3-CAUS-turn.over
'My father turned his own canoe upside down.'

(78) *we*-'yãpema ã-ãpa we-'yn-a
1SG.COR-club 1SG-make 1SG.COR-sit-SER
'I am making my club sitting down.'.

On postpositions the coreferential prefix co-ccurs with the reflexive prefix, as in example 79. In this example, the main verb *'ãpa* 'make', which is transitive, takes the oblique-topicalized form, as indicated by absolutive prefix *i-*.

(79) *a-x(e)*-ewe ã'e ramõ rõ'õ 'yãpema i-'ãpa 'yn-a
3-REFL-DAT DEMON because unattested club 3S-make sit-SER
'It was for himself, because of that, that he was making a club sitting down.'

6.3 Kayabí

The full set of coreferential markers occurs in Kayabí, as described by Dobson (1988), and these are used in all of the syntactic contexts described in Section 4:

te-, oro-, jare-, e-, peje-, o-/w-

On superficial inspection, the *te-* morpheme appears to be unrelated to **wi-*. However it can be explained on the basis of a regularization of a phonological irregularity which occurs with a few morphemes when preceded by **wi-*, as in **wi-t-ekó* '1SG to be (in motion)' : **wi-t-ekó* > *t-ekó* > *te-ekó*.

In subordinate clauses, when O (ex. 80) or S (ex. 81) is coreferential with the subject of the independent clause, the coreferential prefixes are used.

(80) [*o*-ywu re] u'yw-a r-eru-a eru-'a-a
3COR-shoot AFTER arrow LK-bring-TN[26] CC-fall-TN
'After he_2 shot (with arrow) him_1, he_1 fell, bringing down the arrow with $himself_1$.'

(81) [*w*-eweg amõ] o-jo'o-aù-e'em ore-r-a'yr-a
3COR-stomach WH 3-cry-TN-NEG 1EX-LK-child-NC
'Our $children_i$ don't cry when $they_i$ are full-stomached.'

As can be see from example 81, it is permissible in this language for the subject of a subordinate clause to be coreferential with that of the independent clause, unlike Tocantins Asuriní and Tapirapé. The coreferential marking extends as well to the pronominal possessor of the nominal referent of the subordinate verb, as in example 82, where the referent is S.

(82) [*oro*j-a'yr[27] 'ar amũ] kawĩpie apo-ù oro-jo-upe
1IN.COR-child fall WH cooked.cereal make-TN 1IN.COR-REFL-for
'When our_i children are born, we_i make (a special type of) cooked cereal for each other of us_i.'

[26] What Dobson glosses as TN corresponds in form but not in function to the serial verb suffix. In these examples its function seems to more closely correspond to the oblique-topicalized verb form.

[27] According to Dobson, "class B" stems, which appear to be the same as the class II stems in this paper, take the following form: *teje-, oroje- jareje-, eje-, pejeje-,* and *we-*. The *-e* in final position is omitted before a vowel.

In this example, as well as in 80, the verb in the independent clause takes the oblique-topicalized form, and there is no explicit reference to A, which is the trigger for the coreferential marking.

The coreferential prefixes are also used with intransitive serial verbs, as in example 83:

(83) so-o *jare*-jauk-a pej-arþì-a[31] r-upi
1IN-go 1IN.COR-bathe-TN 2PL.COR-grandmother-NC LK-with
'Let's$_i$ go (to the river) to bathe with your$_i$ PL grandmother.'

Coreferential prefixes also occur with nouns. As can be seen in the preceding example, the second person plural referent is coreferential because they are members of the group defined by first person inclusive. The same is true with example 84.

(84) si-juka *ej*-eymaw-a
1IN-kill 2SG.COR-pet
'Let's$_i$ kill your$_i$ SG pet.'

Coreferential prefixes also occur with postpositions, as in example 85, where *o-je-upe*, although occurring in the subordinate clause, is coreferential with the subject of the independent clause.

(85) [era *o*-je-upe t-ur-ypy ramø] n-o-jemi'uar-i
news 3.COR-REFL-to IMPERS-come-INCIP WH NEG-3-eat-NEG
'As soon as the news arrived to her$_i$, she$_i$ didn't eat anymore.'

6.4 Xingu Asuriní

For Xingu Asuriní, which is in the same subgroup as Kayabí, H. da Silva (1995) shows a similar paradigm, including regularization of the first person singular prefix *te-:*

te-, uru-, jare-, e-, pejepe-, u-

Like Kayabí the coreferential marking extends to subordinate clauses, including to the coreferential referent of an intransitive subordinate verb:

(86) ene-peray pe [e-karu-re]
2SG-satisfied INTER 2SG.COR-eat(intransitive)-AFTER
'Were you$_i$ satisfied after you$_i$ ate?'

Intransitive serial verbs also receive coreferential marking, as in examples 87-88:

(87) a-ja'uk *te-a* *te-ka*
1SG-bathe 1SG.COR-go 1SG.COR-be(in motion)
'I am going to bathe.'

---

[28] Data from other languages (Guajajára, Parintintín, Mbyá, and Wayampi) suggest that the *j* should be part of the stem.

(88) sa-tym *sare*-ka
1IN-plant 1IN.COR-be(in motion)
'We are going to plant.'

Coreferential marking with nouns and postpositions are shown in examples 89 and 90, respectively.

(89) a-apa *te*-yara
1SG-make 1SG.COR-canoe
'I made my canoe.'

(90) a-pyyk *te*-je-e
1SG-grasp 1SG.COR-REFL-for
'I grasped it for myself.'

In sum, although some of the above languages may lack some element of the full system, such as coreferential intransitive subordinate verbs in Tocantins Asuriní and possibly Tapirapé, these languages make maximal use of the coreferential prefixes, as indicated in Table 3.

	Subordinate (TV)	**Serial**	**Nominalization**	**Noun (poss.)**	**Postposition**
1 and 2 person	x	x	x	x	x
3 person	x	x	x	x	x

Table 3: Maximal use of coreferential prefixing

In this system the coreferential markers are used in reference to all three persons and in all possible grammatical environments. This system has a high degree of redundancy since coreferential markers are not necessary to disambiguate first and second person referents. However, the coreferential markers bring cohesion to the sentence.

In fact, Dobson (1988:83,89) states for Kayabi that the use of these prefixes goes beyond the sentence level and extends to the "period", which she describes as smaller than a paragraph or episode. Nicholson (1975) also shows that the range of these prefixes extends beyond the sentence for specific discourse purposes. These are on forms derived from serial verbs.

7. Systems in transition

Several languages of the family show signs of being in transition from the more extended system of coreferential marking to a reduced system. This is evident in two different ways: a reduction in the number of syntactic contexts in which cross referencing takes place, beginning with subordinate verbs; and/or the partial or complete substitution of first and second person prefixes from Set 3 by those from Set 2, or by a combination of those from Set 2 and

Set 1, depending on the syntactic context. In this section I will not necessarily give complete data for each language, but will show the principle evidence of its transitional status.

7.1 Kamaiurá

Kamaiurá, from subgroup 7, has the full set of coreferential markers:
we-, oro-, jere-, e-, peje-, o-

However, they are not used as fully in this language as they are in the "maximal use" languages. In example 91 we would expect S of the subordinate clause to be coreferential because it is identical with A in the main clause (Seki 1983), but the prefix *je-* from Set 2, not Set 3, is used.

(91) [*je* akajym -amoẽ] oro-ekat
1SG worry-WH 1A+2SG.O-search.for
'When I got worried I looked for you SG.'

Seki (1989) describes the set of coreferential prefixes as being characteristic of dependent intransitive serial verbs (which she calls gerunds), and gives a complete paradigm for both agentive (example 92) and non-agentive (example 93).

(92)	a-jot	*we*-maraka-m	'I come, singing'
	oro-jot	*oro*-maraka-m	'we EX come, singing'
	ja-jot	*jere*-maraka-m	'we IN come, singing'
	ere-jot	*e*-maraka-m	'you SG come, singing'
	pe-jot	*peje*-maraka-m	'you PL come, singing'
	o-jot	*o*-maraka-m	'[3] come(s), singing'

(93)	a-jot	*we*-katu-ram	'I come to be good'
	oro-jot	*oro*-katu-ram	'we EX come to be good'
	ja-jot	*jere*-katu-ram	'we IN come to be good'
	ere-jot	*e*-katu-ram	'you SG come to be good'
	pe-jot	*peje*-katu-ram	'you PL come to be good'
	o-jot	*o*-katu-ram	'[3] come(s) to be good'

She also gives an example (1990:379) of the third person coreferential prefix on nouns, as in example 94.

(94) *o*-nami-a o-kutuk
3COR-ear-NC 3-pierce
'He pierced his (own) ear.'

However, in example 95, where we would normally expect a first person singular coreferential prefix to occur with the nominalized form of a transitive verb, the Set 2 prefix *je-* is used.

(95) a-kwahaw-in *je* kyci-taw-a
1SG-know-IRREAL 1SG cut-NOM-NC
'I know that you will cut me.' (Lit. '....my (being) cut')

It would appear that coreferential marking has not been eliminated altogether outside the context of serial verbs, but is limited to third person, which would raise the possibility that it exists as well for third person in temporal subordinate clauses (parallel to sentence 89).

7.2 Parintintín

Parintintín has a modified set of cross-referencing prefixes:
i-, oro-, nhande-, e-, pe(ji)-, o-

Two plural forms have been replaced by person markers from Set 2: first person inclusive **jere-* by *nhande-(/jane/)* and **peje-* by *pe-*, as demonstrated in Table 4.

Parintintin Set 3	*Set 2	*Set 3
i-	*čé	**wi-*
oro-	*oré	**oro-*
nhande-	**jané*	*jere-
e-	*né	**e-*
pe-	**pé*	*peje-
o-	**i-*	*o-

Table 4: Substitution of forms in Parintintín paradigm

However, in personal communication Pease says that the Parintintín, as well as their close relatives, the Tenharim, often use *peji-* instead of *pe-* on a intransitive verb of 'construction 3', which I refer to as a dependent serial verb. She gives as an example: *peji-kyhyji-avo* 'being afraid'. She also states that in Tenharim *ji-* is used instead of *i-* for first person inclusive; this is the same as the Parintintín reflex of **čé* from Set 2. Thus Tenharim is one step beyond Parintintín in the replacement process.

The coreferential prefixes are used in Parintintín to indicate the subject of agentive or non-agentive verbs in a serial verb construction, and to indicate the possessor of a noun which is coreferential with the subject of the clause (Betts 1981). She also states that the reflexive prefix *ji-* occurs together with this prefix set in postpositional phrases. According to Pease (p.c.) this prefix set also occurs in temporal subordinate clauses when the referent, S of an intransitive verb or O of a transitive verb, is coreferential with the subject of the main clause, or at least that this pattern was in place with their middle-aged language helper. She observed that their language helper's son did not seem to be so concerned about coreferential agreement in subordinate clauses, and that the Tenharim seem to be losing coreferential agreement in this context. It was her impression that coreferential marking is less likely in preposed subordinate clauses than in postposed ones.

Based on the modifications to the prefix set, we can say that the degree of change is more or less comparable to Kamaiurá, though different.

7.3 Tupinambá

Tupinambá, from subgroup 3, also has a modified set of coreferential prefixes. In the following paradigm, the coreferential forms **jere-* and **peje-* have both been replaced by the equivalent forms from Set 1:

we-, oro-, ja-, e-, pe-, o-

Although cross referencing on subordinate verbs in Tupinambá is absolutive, providing the appropriate environment for the coreferential markers, Rodrigues, who is very thorough in his description, does not make any reference to their occurrence in this construction.

The fullest set of coreferential markers in Tupinambá occur with agentive intransitive serial verbs (S_a), called *gerúndios* by Rodrigues, as in the following paradigm (Rodrigues 1953) of the verb 'to laugh':[29]

(96)	*wi*-puká-βo	'and I laughed'
	oro-puká-βo	'and we EX laughed'
	ja-puká-βo	'and we IN laughed'
	e-puká-βo	'and you SG laughed'
	pe-puká-βo	'and you PL laughed'
	o-puká-βo	'and [3] laughed'

In nonagentive intransitive serial verbs (S_o), only the third person coreferential prefix occurs. The rest of the paradigm shows Set 2 person markers, as in example 97:

(97)	*sjé* katú-ramo	'I, being good'
	oré katú-ramo	'we EX, being good'
	jané katú-ramo	'we IN, being good'
	né katú-ramo	'you SG, being good'
	pé katú-ramo	'you PL, being good'
	o-katú-ramo	'[3-COR], being good'

The use of *wi-* and *e-* is so restricted that Rodrigues does not describe them as part of a set with the third person coreferential prefix *o-* at all. In fact, he describes the set of prefixes occurring in agentive intransitive dependent serial verbs as being Nominative 2, varying in form from Nominative 1 (i.e. Set 1 system), and describes *wi-* and *e-* as allomorphs of *a-* and *ere-,* respectively

[29] I have updated the orthography which Rodrigues used in 1953 to reflect his later conclusions about Tupinamba phonemes.

(1981). This is not surprising, since the Tupinambá was in the process of substituting Set 1 prefixes for those of Set 3 in the one context in which any reflexes of first and second coreferential person markers still occurred, i.e., the serial verbs. Thus, the split-S system which already occurred in independent verbs is extended in this language to the context of dependent serial verbs: the nonagentive verbs taking Set 2 (S/O) person markers for first and second person, and the agentive intransitive verbs taking Set 1 (A/S) markers, as demonstrated in Table 5.

Tupinambá Set 3	***Set 1**	***Set 3**
wi-	*a-	**wi-*
oro-	**oro-*	**oro-*
ja-	**ja-*	*jere-
e-	*ere-	**e-*
pe-	**pe-*	*peje-
o-	**o-*	**o-*

Table 5: Tupinambá paradigm for agentive intransitive dependent serial verbs, in transition from Set 3 to Set 1

Note that the prefixes **oro-* and **o-* occur in both Set 1 and 3. Therefore all that is necessary for these two prefixes is a reinterpretation of set membership.

Just as it occurs with nonagentive intransitive serial verbs, the third person coreferential prefix *o-* occurs with nouns. For example, from the dictionary of Dias (1965):[30]

(98) *o*-sý o-werekó *o*-irø-namo
3COR-mother 3A-have 3COR-companion-as
'He had his (COR) mother with him (lit. as his (COR) companion).'

This prefix also occurs with postpositions, as can be seen in the following examples from Barbosa's dictionary (1970) (hyphens added):

(99) *o-je*-pupé reflexive form of the postposition *pupé* 'in'
o-je-upé reflexive form of the postposition *supé* 'to, at'
o-jo-upé reciprocal and reflexive form of *supé* 'to himself, to each other'

In sum, Tupinambá shows a greater reduction of the coreferential marking stem than either Kamaiurá or Parintintín: not only is the number of forms which are reflexes of the Proto-Set 3 reduced, the environment in which they occur is also reduced. Reflexes of **wi-* and **e-* occur only with agentive of intransitive dependent serial verbs, and not with nonagentive verbs. Reflexes **jere-* and **peje-* do not occur at all.

[30] I have rewritten Dias' examples to make them consistent with Rodrigues' current spelling, for purposes of clarification.

7.4 Guarayu

An even greater reduction of the coreferential set can be seen in agentive intransitive serial verbs in Guarayu, a member of subgroup 2 (Newton 1978, and in personal communication). Whereas Tupinambá replaced the first and second plural coreferential prefixes with Set 1 prefixes but retained their singular counterparts, Guarayu took this substitution process one step further, replacing **e-* with *ere-*. This leaves only one prefix which gives any clue that the cross referencing system in this syntactic context was ever anything other than Set 1: *vi-* (<**wi-* 1SG), as can be seen by the paradigm in example 100. Since its occurrence is restricted to serial verbs, *vi-* cannot very easily be defined in this language as a coreferential prefix. (Note that in this language the serial verb suffix has also been deleted.)

(100) a-jevy *vi*-t-u[31] 'I came back (returned, coming)'
oro-jevy *oro*-ju 'we EX came back (returned, coming)'
ja-jevy *ja*-ju 'we IN came back (returned, coming)'
ere-jevy *ere*-ju 'you SG came back (returned, coming)'
pe-jevy *pe*-ju 'you PL came back (returned, coming)'
o-jevy *o*-u '[3] came back (returned, coming)'

In Guarayu the temporal subordinate clause marker **-(r)VmV* 'when' has been replaced by a suffix *-se.*[32] Cross referencing on verbs combining with *-se* is like that on independent verbs, to a large degree eliminating the environment in which the coreferential markers might occur. In example 101 the subordinate verb is marked by *o-*, which must be from Set 1, since its referent is the jaguar, and therefore not coreferential with the subject of the independent verb, fox.

(101) [jawar o-jevy-se *w*-etã-ve[33] o-so] a'ese aipo aware o-jẽ'ẽ
jaguar 3-return-WH 3COR-home-at 3-go then HRSY fox 3-speak

uruvu upe
vulture to

'When the jaguar returned (going) to his (own) house, then the fox spoke to the vulture.'

Guarayu retains use of only the third person coreferential prefix with nouns (ex. 102). With other persons, the Set 2 person markers are used, as in

[31] This stem is irregular (throughout the language family). With Set 1 markers the *ju* *(<*júr)* allomorph occurs with first and second person, and the *u (<*úr)* allomorph occurs with third person. The *t-* is an irregularity which appears under certain circumstances, including following the first person Set 3 marker **wi-*.

[32] Perhaps from the Spanish *se* 'if'?

[33] In several languages, *w-* occurs as an allomorph of the **o-* morpheme before certain vowels.

example 103.

(102) o-mbopa aipo *o*-mianga avei
3-deceive (hearsay) 3COR-uncle also
'He also deceived his (own) uncle again.'

(103) a'e *če* py'a pype
I.say 1SG heart in
'I say in my heart.'

As in other languages, the coreferential form of postpositions requires the use of the reflexive prefix *je-* (ex.104).

(104) ja-s-eka rãnå yvyra *jande*-je-upe
1IN-3-search first wood 1SG-REFL-for
'First we search for wood for ourselves.'

The third person coreferential prefix is used with third person: *o-je-upe* (Newton, p.c.).

7.5 Guajajára and Tembé

In Guajajára and Tembé, members of the Tenetehára cluster of subgroup 4, the only regularly occurring coreferential prefix is the third person prefix, *u-/o-*, which occurs in nearly all of the traditional syntactic environments. First and second person coreferential prefixes are replaced by person markers from Set 2. The degree of reduction in these languages is a major difference from the other languages in the same subgroup, which retain a full set of coreferential markers (Sections 6.1 and 6.2).

Temporal subordinate clauses retain the absolutive cross-referencing system. A coreferential distinction is indicated with intransitive verbs when the subject is third person (as in examples 105 and 106, agentive and nonagentive, respectively).

(105)a) [*i*-ho mehe] u-zai'o a'e 'When he [nonCOR] went he cried.'
3-go WH 3-cry 3A

b) [*o*-ho mehe] u-zai'o a'e 'When he [COR] went he cried.'
3COR-go WH 3-cry 3S

(106)a)[*h*-urywete mehe] u-zegar a'e 'When he was happy he [nonCOR] sang.'
3-happy WH 3-sing 3S

b) [(*u*-)urywete mehe] u-zegar a'e 'When he was happy he [COR] sang.'
3COR-happy WH 3-sing 3S

It is also correct to use coreferential prefixing on a transitive subordinate verb when the O is coreferential with the subject of the main clause, as in example 107. However, there is a resistance toward using this construction (Harrison and N. da Silva, personal communication). It is preferable to detransitivize the verb by using the reflexive prefix and to put the information in a sequence of independent clauses instead of using subordination (ex. 108).

(107)a) [i-petek mehe] u-zai'o 'when X hit him/her [nonCOR] he/she cried'
3-hit WH 3-cry

b) [u-petek mehe] u-zai'o 'when X hit him/her [COR] he/she cried'
3COR-hit WH 3-cry

(108) U-ze-kixi. A'e rupi u-zai'o.
3-REFL-cut Therefore 3-cry
'He cut himself. Therefore he cried.'

Likewise in dependent serial verbs Set 2 prefixes are used for first or second person, and the coreferential prefix is used for third. This is true for both agentive and nonagentive intransitive verbs. Agentive serial verbs (ex. 109) take the suffix *-pà*. Nonagentive ones (ex. 110-111) may take either *-pà* or *-romo*.

(109) uru-zuka *ne*-mugwaw-pà 'I'll kill you, making you fall.'
1EX-kill 2SG-make.fall-SER

(110) a-zypyrog *he*-r-urywete-pà 'I began to be happy.'
OR a-zypyrog *he*-r-urywete-romo
1SG-begin 1SG-LK-happy-SER

(111) u-zypyrog (*u*-)urywete-pà 'He began to be happy.'
OR u-zypyrog (*u*-)urywete-romo
3-begin 3COR-happy-SER

Certain verbs have developed into auxiliary verbs, which occur without *pà*. One of these is *ho* 'to go' which occurs with Set 1 prefixes instead of Set 2. Whereas example 112 is grammatically correct, 113 is more natural.

(112) ere-ho *ne*-ker-pà 'You SG are going to sleep.'
(113) a-ker *a*-ho 'I am going to sleep.'

Coreferentiality with a third person subject is indicated on postposition by a combination of the reflexive prefix *ze-* with the Set 3 coreferential prefix *u-*. When the stem of the postposition is reduplicated and a plural subject is indicated by the *wà* morpheme, the first interpretation is reciprocal, as in example 114.

(114) u-pyhyk *i*-zupe a'e 'he grasped it for him [nonCOR]'
u-pyhyk *u-ze*-upe a'e 'he grasped it for himself'
u-pyhyk *u-ze*-upe-upe a'e wà 'they grasped it/them for each other'

For first and second persons coreferential referencing is indicated by a person marker from Set 2 plus the reflexive prefix, as in example 115.

(115) a-pyhyk *he-ze*-upe[34] ihe 'I grasped it for myself'

Nouns also receive coreferential marking only with third person, as in 116.

(116) u-pyhyk *i*-ma'e a'e 'he grasped/grabbed his [nonCOR] thing'
u-pyhyk *u*-ma'e a'e 'he grasped/grabbed his (own) thing'
a-pyhyk *he*-ma'e ihe 'I grasped./grabbed my (own) thing'

In sum, languages in transition range from having a full set of coreferential prefixes (Kamaiurá) to having only a third person prefix (Guajajára). In combination with nouns and postpositions, the first and second person prefixes are replaced by person markers from Set 2, which in postpositional phrases co-occur with the reflexive (or reciprocal) prefix, as illustrated in Table 6:

	Set 2		*Set 3*
1SG	*čé	>	*~~wi~~-
1EX	*oré	>	*~~oro~~-
1IN	*jané	>	*~~jere~~-
2SG	*né	>	*~~e~~-
2PL	*pé	>	*~~peje~~-
3			*o-

Table 6: Paradigm replacement on nouns and postpositions

On verbs the first and second person prefixes are replaced either by Set 1 prefixes or by Set 2 prefixes, as illustrated in Table 7:

	Set 1		**Set 3**	**Set 3**		**Set 2**
	A/S		**COR O/S**	**COR O/S**		**O/S**
1SG	*a-	>	*wi-	*wi-	<	*čé
1EX	*oro-	=	(*oro-)	*oro-	<	*oré
1IN	*ja-	>	*jere-	*jere-	<	*jané
2SG	*ere-	>	*e-	*e-	<	*né
2PL	*pe-	>	*peje-	*peje-	<	*pé
3	*o-	=	(*o)-	*o-		

Table 7: Paradigm replacement on subordinate and dependent serial verbs

---

[34] The non-coreferential equivalent of this sentence does not use the postposition *upe*, but rather the dative form *-we*, as in the following example: *u-pyhyk he-we a'e* 'he grasped it for me.'

When the prefixes on verbs are replaced by Set 2 markers, the **oro-* prefix naturally changes to **ore,* but the **o-* prefix is retained as a coreferential prefix. When the prefixes are replaced by Set 1 prefixes, the **oro-* and **o-* prefixes are reinterpreted as part of the Set 1 paradigm, resulting in a complete elimination of coreferential marking in this syntactic context. This is indicated by an = sign in the table. The first place where coreferential marking is likely to be eliminated is in the cross referencing on subordinate verbs.

Comparative paradigms of intransitive serial verbs suggest that paradigm replacement is a gradual process. The data in Table 9 are arranged by degree of paradigm replacement.

	Set 3	**Kamaiurá**	**Parintintín**	**Tupinambá**	**Guarayú**	**Guajajára**
1SG	*wi-	we-	i-	wi-	vi-	he-
1EX	*oro-	oro-	oro-	oro-	oro-	ore-
1IN	*jere-	jere-	jane-	ja-	ja-	zane-
2SG	*e-	e-	e-	e-	ere-	ne-
2PL	*peje-	peje-	pe-	pe-	pe-	pe-
3	*o-	o-	o-	o-	o-	o-
Direction of change:			*O/S*	*A/S*	*A/S*	*O/S*

Table 8: Paradigm replacement in transition - serial verbs

As can be seen from the table, Kamaiurá (Seki 1989), from subgroup 7, has the full set of coreferential prefixes, whereas Guajajára (Harrison 1986 and p.c.), from subgroup 4, retains only the third-person form. Parintintín, member of subgroup 6, has undergone a partial substitution by person markers from Set 2 (Betts 1981). Like Parintintín, Guajajára has undergone replacement of coreferential forms by those of Set 2, retaining the absolutive cross-referencing system along with the third person coreferential prefix *o-*. In Tupinambá (Rodrigues 1953), from subgroup 3, and Guarayu (Newton 1978), from subgroup 2, the coreferential prefixing on dependent intransitive serial verbs has been partially replaced by forms from the nominative set (Set 1), with Guarayu being further along in the substitution process than Tupinambá. The *o-* and *oro-* prefixes are not distinguishable from those of the replacement set and can no longer be considered coreferential markers.

8. Minimal system

Another set of languages, including Wayampi and the Guaraní subgroup, makes minimal use of the coreferential markers. Only the third person form is used, which is the only one which is really necessary to disambiguate referents. Furthermore, the degree of ergativity has been significantly reduced in these languages, reducing the environment in which the coreferential marker could occur.

8.1 Wayampi

In Wayampi[35] subordinate verbs, the same system of verbal agreement is used as with independent verbs. That is, a person hierarchy is used with transitive verbs (ex. 117-118), subject prefixes from Set 1 are used for agentive intransitive verbs (ex. 119), and person markers from Set 2 are used for non-agentive transitive verbs. The use of coreferential markers does not extend to subordinate clauses, even i n the case of the nonagentive verbs, as can be seen by the form *i-katu-pa* instead of *o-katu-pa* in example 120.

(117) [o-erekwa *o*-juka rem ẽ] o-o
3COR-wife 3-kill WH 3-go
'When he killed his wife, he went.'

(118) [*e*-r-eity *eipa* remẽ ipe] ywa o-'a-ta
1SG-LK-drop 2A COND FUTIL sky 3-fall-FUT
'If you drop me, the sky will fall.'

(119) [amã *o*-ky remẽ te] o-je'ẽ
rain 3-rain WH EMPH 3-call
'It (curassow bird) calls only when it's raining.'

(120) [*i*-katu-pa remẽ] o-jywy o-o
3-good-COMPL WH 3-return 3-go
'When he$_i$ got well, he$_i$ returned going.'

Agentive intransitive serial verbs occur with subject prefixes from Set 1. Since the third person prefix for Set 1 is identical with that of the coreferential prefix in Set 3, the prefix in this context is no longer identifiable as coreferential, as in example 121. On the rare occasions that nonagentive intransitive verbs occur as dependent serial verbs, the coreferential prefix *o-* does occur, as in example 122.

(121) a-jywy *a*-a 'I returned, going'
o-jywy *o*-o 'he returned, going'

(122) n-a-a-i, e'i *o*-wari ramõ
NEG-1SG-go-NEG 3.say 3COR-lie SER
'I didn't go, he said lying.'

Only the third person coreferential marker is used with nouns to refer to a coreferential possessor, as in example 123. This includes nominalizations, as in example 124.

---

[35] Data in this paper is from the Jari dialect of Wayampi.

(123) a-a *e*-y resa 'I went to see my mother'
a-a *i*-(j)y resa 'I went to see his mother [nonCOR]'
o-o *o*-y resa 'he went to see his own mother [COR]'

(124) o-o *o*-mo'e-are r-esa
3-go 3COR-teach-NOM.FORMER LK-see
'He went to see his (own) former teacher.'

The coreferential prefix also occurs with postpositions, as in ex. 125.

(125) marija a pyy *e*-upe 'I bought a knife for myself'
marija a-pyy *i*-(j)upe 'I bought a knife for him'
marija o-pyy *o*-upe 'he bought a knife for himself'

Unlike the other Tupí-Guaraní languages, in Wayampi the *o*- attaches directly to the postposition without the use of the reflexive prefix *je*- to give a coreferential meaning. If the *je*- is used with the postposition, it has a reciprocal meaning, as in example 126.

(126) marija o-pyy *o-je*-upe kupa
knife 3-buy 3COR-REFL-for PL
' They bought knives for each other.'

It appears that the use of this form with *o*-, which originally just indicated third person, has been extended to occur with first and second person as well.

8.2 Mbyá Guaraní

Like Wayampi Mbyá Guaraní retains only the third person coreferential prefix. This is unlike Old Guaraní (D. Rodrigues 1997), which retained the *wi*- and *e*- prefixes with intransitive serial verbs, like Tupinambá.

Like Wayampi, subordinate verbs receive the same cross referencing as in independent verbs, as in example 127, and therefore are not targets for coreferential prefixing.

(127) [*a*-porandu ramo] o-mbovai
1SG-ask WH 3-answer
'When I asked, he answered.'

Dooley (1992:98) reports a switch-reference marking mechanism in temporal subordinate clauses: *vy* (derived from the serial verb suffix **-áβo*) for same subject (SS) reference, and *ramõ* (from the simultaneous/conditional morpheme **-(r)VmV*) or *rã* for different (DS) reference, as in example 128.

(128) a) [ava o-o vy] moi o-exa
man 3-go SS snake 3-see
'When the man went, he saw the snake.'

b) [ava o-o ramõ] moi o-exa
man 3-go DS snake 3-see
'When the man went, the snake saw him.'

Independent intransitive serial verbs no longer use the coreferential set of prefixes. As in Wayampi, these have been replaced by those of Set 1, as in example 129, thus eliminating the environment for coreferential marking.

(129) a-jevy *a*-ju-vy
1SG-return 1SG-come-SER
'I returned, coming'

According to Dooley (p.c.) this type of construction does not occur with nonagentive intransitive verbs.

The third person coreferential prefix is retained in combination with nouns, as in example 130.[36]

(130) o-jevy *o*-yvy py
3-return 3COR-land to
'He returned to his own land.'

The third person coreferential prefix also occurs on a postpositions (in combination with the reflexive prefix *je*-), as in example 131.

(131) *o-je*-upe aipo e'i
3COR-REFL-to DEMON 3.say
'He said like that to himself.'

Dooley also reports *o-jo-upe* 'to each other'. Whenever the argument of the postposition refers to the subject the reflexive prefix is used, but for first and second persons it combines with person markers of Set 2, as in example 132.

(132) a-poraei *xe-je*-upe
1SG-sing 1SG-REFL-to
'I sang to myself.'

In sum, these languages make minimal use of coreferential cross referencing, as shown in Table 9. Coreferential prefixes for first and second persons have been eliminated, thus eliminating the redundancy of the system where it is not necessary for disambiguation. Furthermore, the occurrence of the third person coreferential marker has been severely reduced on verbs, due to the reduction of the environment (absolutive) in which they could occur.

---

[36] Presumably there is some restriction of coreferential marking on nominalizations, since in Mbyá and other Guaranian languages the nominalizations of circumstance take the same prefixing as independent verbs (Jensen 1990:144,145).

	Subordinate V	Serial (IV) S_a or S_o	Nominalization	Noun (poss.)	Postposition
1 and 2 person					
3 person		(x)	x	x	x

Table 9: Minimal use of coreferential prefixing

The motivation for this elimination of coreferential marking on verbs is the elimination of the morphosyntactic environment in which the prefixing originally occurred. As mentioned above, the coreferential prefixing occurred in the context of absolutive cross referencing. In the original system, the potential environment for coreferential prefixing includes subordinate verb and intransitive serial verbs, as indicated by italics in Table 10. Transitive serial verbs, which cross reference O, do not receive coreferential prefixing because it is A that is identical with the subject of the main verb.

	Independent	Subordinate	Dependent serial
Intransitive	Split-S	*Absolutive (S)*	*Absolutive (S)*
Transitive	Split ergative	*Absolutive (O)*	Absolutive (O)

Table 10: Cross-referencing in Proto-Tupí-Guaraní

In Wayampi subordinate verbs, the same system of verbal agreement is used as with independent verbs. That is, a person hierarchy is used with transitive verbs, subject prefixes from Set 1 are used for agentive intransitive verbs, and person markers from Set 2 are used for nonagentive transitive verbs. This system has also been extended to intransitive serial verbs. These cross-referencing changes have resulted in the elimination of the environments in which the coreferential marking originally occurred, as in Table 11.

	Independent	Subordinate	Dependent serial
Intransitive	Split-S	*Split-S*	*Split-S* (S_a / S_o)
Transitive	Split ergative	*Split ergative*	Absolutive (O)

Table 11: Cross-referencing in Wayampi

9. Eliminated system

In Urubu-Kaapor even the third person coreferential prefix has been eliminated. This is just one aspect of a major simplification of the overall person-marker system that has taken place in this language. Only Set 1 prefixes occur with transitive and agentive intransitive verbs, creating a strictly nominative-accusative system (Jensen 1990). Even nominalizations receive the Set 1 rather than Set 2 person markers. The underlined verb in example 133 is a subordinate intransitive verb, and the one in 134 is an intransitive serial verb. In both cases the S_a is coreferential with the subject of the main verb, but no coreferential marking is used because the environment in which it occurred (i.e. replacing Set 2 person markers) has been eliminated.

(133) ajame'ẽ ke [marajã ngi ihẽ a-hyk rahã]
after.that EMPH Maranhão from I 1SG-arrive WH

mataru rehe ihẽ a-sak tĩ
Mataru on/at I 1SG-see again
'After that, when I arrived back from Maranhão, I saw Mataru again.'

(134) ihẽ riki wewe katu a-jur a-xo
I EMPH slowly good 1 SG-come 1SG-move
'I was coming very slowly.'

Only Set 2 person markers occur with nonagentive intransitive verbs, nouns, and postpositions. Sets 3 and 4 have been eliminated altogether. Consequently there is no longer a way, even on nouns, to disambiguate whether a referent is coreferential. In examples 135 and 136 the same form is used for 'his wife', *h-akehar*, even though the referent of 'his' is coreferential with the subject in 125 and non-coreferential in 135, since in the latter it is a prefix on the subject itself. The prefix *h- (<*c),* from Set 2, occurs with both.

(135) pe kuja pytun mokõi pytun pe h-akehar rehe o-ho tĩ
and like.this night two night then 3-wife LK-for 3-go also
'And after this many nights, two nights, he went for his wife also.'

(136) ere-rur aja je h-akehar pandu i-pe
2SG bring thus HRSY 3-wife 3+say 3-to
'"Did you bring it?" thus, it is said, his wife said to him.'

The only area in which coreferentiality is still clearly indicated morphologically is in the postpositions. However, it is the reflexive/reciprocal prefix *ju-* that indicates its coreferentiality with the subject. The third person coreferential prefix **o-* has been replaced by the normal prefix *i-*, although this does not always occur. Example 137 is a normal form, and the examples in 138 are coreferential.

(137) *i*-pe 'to him' non-coreferential

(138) *ju*-pe 'to himself'
ihẽ ju-pe 'to myself' } coreferential
jande ju-pe 'to ourselves'

The elimination of the coreferential prefixes in Urubu-Kaapor is exemplified by an empty table:

	Subordinate V	Serial (IV) S_a or S_o	Nominalization	Noun (poss.)	Postposition
1 and 2 person					
3 person					

Table 12: Coreferential prefixing nonexistent

10. Conclusions

To summarize the coreferential cross referencing in Tupí-Guaraní languages, those which make maximal use of the system have a high degree of grammaticalized cohesion, but are also redundant, since coreferential markers for first and second person are not necessary for purposes of disambiguation. When first and second persons are eliminated on nouns and postpositions, they are substituted with person markers from Set 2. When they are eliminated on verbs, there is a choice between the person markers from Set 1 (A/S) and the ones from Set 2 (S/O), and this choice is partly related to a decrease in the extent of the ergative-absolutive cross-referencing system. If the Set 3 prefixes are replaced by the forms from Set 2, the coreferential prefix for third person is usually retained. If they are replaced by the Set 1 forms, the third person prefix *o-* is reinterpreted as the homonymous prefix from that set for lack of contrast. The underlying nominative-accusative system, as evidenced on the syntactic level by the trigger of the coreferential marking system, is no doubt a principal motivator in the systematic replacement of absolutive person markers by nominative prefixes in the languages of subgroups 1 and 8 (see Jensen 1990). Where this has happened the number of structures in which coreferential marking can occur is reduced, making them "minimal use" languages. Languages which fall in the transitional category allow us to get a glimpse of these changes taking place. They serve as a reminder that changes from one system to another are not made overnight, but rather are a gradual process. And the data from Urubu-Kaapor is a reminder that ultimately a system, such as Set 3, can be eliminated altogether.

The behavior of various languages in regard to coreferential marking is summarized, by subgroup, in Table 13.

1	Minimal use	Mybá Guaraní.
2	Transitional	Guarayu.
3	Transitional	Tupinambá (extinct).
4	Maximal use Transitional	Tocantins Asuriní. Tapirapé. Tenetehára cluster (Guajajára, Tembé).
5	Maximal use	Xingu Asuriní. Kayabí. **Araweté??**
6	Transitional	Parintintín. Tenharim.
7	Transitional	Kamaiurá
8	Eliminated Minimal use	Urubu-Kaapor. Wayampi.

Table 13: Cross referencing by subgroup

In the proposed subgroup 4, languages from the Akwawa cluster, as well as Tapirapé, show a complete set of coreferential markers which is used in broad syntactic circumstances. In contrast, all five first and second person markers have been eliminated in Guajajára and Tembé. I suggest that this difference is sufficient reason to reconsider whether the Tenetehára cluster should be a separate subgroup. There are two phonological features which also show its distance from the other languages of the subgroup. The Tenetehára cluster does not show the same kind of vowel shift that is characteristic of Tapirapé and the Akwawa cluster. The principal vocalic change in Guajajára is the creation of an additional vowel by the failure of the reflexes of **a* and **ã* to merge when nasalization was eliminated. Another difference is that Guajajára and Tembé retain the reflex of **j* as a distinct phoneme, which did not merge with the reflexes of **pj*, the palatalized allophone of **t*, and other sources, as in Tapirapé and the Akwára cluster.

I also suggest that information about the coreferential system be included in the criteria for proving or disproving the subgrouping of Arawete, which Rodrigues has very tentatively placed in subgroup 5, together with Kayabí and Xingu Asuriní. Since the other languages of this subgroup show maximal use of the coreferential system and the regularization of *te-* as a first person marker, we would expect to find something similar in Arawete if it is a member of the same subgroup.

11. Further questions

11.1 The origins of coreferential prefixes

Rodrigues (1985) has prepared a list of 121 cognates between Tupí and the

Carib language family. These include five personal affixes, among them the two reconstructed for Tupí-Guaraní as first and second person singular coreferential prefixes: **wi-* and **e-*, respectively. Thus, although they apparently did not always have the meaning of coreferentiality, they nevertheless have existed as morphemes for a very long time. The reflexive prefix, which is reconstructed in Proto-Tupí-Guaraní as **je-* is also in the list of cognates.

Two other prefixes, **oro-* '1EX' and **o-* '3', are identical with prefixes from Set 1.

The two remaining prefixes, **jere-* '1IN' and **peje-* '2PL', are the most difficult to explain. They do not seem to have a history as long as **wi-* and **e-*, nor do they occur in as many languages. In Tupinambá, which retains *wi-* and *e-*, *ja-* occurs instead of **jere-* and *pe-* occurs instead of **peje-*. Both of the prefixes in this language coincide with the prefixes in Set 1. Parintintín retains *i-* (< **wi-*) and *e-*. The Set 2 person markers *nhande-* (/*jane*/ occurs in place of **jere-*, although Pease says (p.c.) that she has observed some use of *jare-* in Tenharim, and *pe-* occurs in place of **peje-*, although *peji-* has not been completely eliminated. Although **jere-* and **peje-* are longer than their counterparts in Set 1, they are the same length (bi-syllabic) as the comparable independent pronouns **jané* and **pe...ẽ*. Reflexes of these two prefixes occur in Tocantins Asuriní and Tapirapé, both from subgroup 4; Kayabí and Xingu Assuriní, both from subgroup 5; and Kamaiurá, from subgroup 7. Phonological changes in these three subgroups do not mark them as being more closely related to each other than to other subgroups, so it would be hard to explain these two morphemes as later developments among a group of more closely-related languages. Moreover, I do not see any way of explaining these forms as independent developments in the various languages. It might be possible to argue for the derivation of **pejé* from **pe-* '2PL' + **je-* 'reflexive', but since this still leaves the **jere-* form unaccounted for, I do not see any advantage to this analysis.

11.2 The range in coreferential rules

Another question is the range of coreferential rules in Proto-Tupí-Guaraní languages. In this paper I have shown that in some languages the subordinate verb receives a coreferential prefix when its referent (S of intransitive verbs or O of transitive verbs) is coreferential with the subject (A or S) of the independent clause. In fact, in Kayabí and in Tocantins Asuriní there is evidence (not cited in this paper) that the use of the coreferential prefixing extends even beyond the sentence, assuming a significant discourse level function. According to Dobson (1988:83), "a reflexive (i.e. coreferential) pronoun in Kayabí which indicates coreference with the subject of the main clause can occur in any place in the period (larger than a sentence), even in the subordinate clause. In other words, in Kayabí, the range of the reflexivity (i.e. cross-referencing) is the period, and not the clause, unlike many other languages." Nicholson (1975) says that in Tocantins Asuriní, initiating (i.e. independent) verbs are used in longer discourses to express the main points of the plot. Backgrounding, including minor events, is expressed through the non-initiating verbs which are related morphologically to dependent serial verbs in other languages, but occur beyond the range of the clause. If the verb is intransitive, the Set 3 coreferential markers are used. This type of verb is also used for the conclusions to sections. Thus in two languages, at least, coreferential marker goes beyond the range of the sentence and is used for discourse purposes.

In other languages, such as Tupinambá and Kamaiurá, the set of coreferential markers seems to be most closely identified with intransitive dependent serial verbs, with no evidence that they occur beyond the clause. Such a difference in the range of the coreferential markers creates questions about the extent of the system in Proto-Tupí-Guaraní. There is enough evidence from various languages of their occurrence with subordinate verbs that it seems safe to reconstruct their usage in the proto-language. However, to reconstruct their function on their discourse level would be more questionable. Nevertheless, their function on this level in two languages from separate subgroups forces us to recognize that there are some major differences in discourse strategy within the language family, between those languages which have extended use of coreferential markers and those that do not. More detailed conclusions would require a separate study and a separate paper.

Acknowledgments

In a way field linguists are like explorers. The prospect of studying a language never before studied holds great excitement, even more so if the language is unrelated to any other language. But working with a language which belongs to a family in which extensive fieldwork has already been done has its own potential for excitement. I began doing comparative work in the Tupí-Guaraní family in 1978 and am still surprised and excited by the discovery of new treasures which help to make the linguistic history of this family unfold. One of the treasures I discovered while working on this paper is the *vi-* suffix in Guarayu, placing this language beyond Tupinambá in a progression of change. I am grateful to all the Tupí-Guaraní linguists whose works have made comparative work possible and to their indigenous language helpers. I am particularly thankful to Heliana da Silva, Norval da Silva, Rose Dobson, Bob Dooley, Floriano Guajajára, Carl Harrison, Jim Kakumasu, Dennis

Newton, Helen Pease, and Auristéa Souza e Silva for provision or clarification of data through personal communication; to Yonne Leite for first stimulating my interest in this area when we participated in the Working Conference for Amazonian Languages held at the University of Oregon in August 1987 (funded by grants from NSF: BNS-8617854, NEH: RX-20870-87, and the University of Oregon Foundation); and to Alexandra Aichenvald, Bob Dooley, and Carl Harrison for their constructive criticism of earlier versions of this paper.

References

Barbosa, Padre A. Lemos. 1970. Pequeno vocabulário Português-Tupi. Rio de Janeiro: Livraria São José.

Bendor-Samuel, David. 1972. Hierarchical structures in Guajajara. Norman: Summer Institute of Linguistics.

Betts, La Vera. 1981. Dicionário Parintintín-Português Português-Parintintín. Brasilia: Summer Institute of Linguistics.

da Silva, Heliana Maria. 1995. Marcadores de pessoa na língua Asuriní do Xingu. Senior monograph prepared for the Federal University of Pará (Brazil).

Dias, Gonçalves. 1965. Dicionário da língua Tupi. Rio de Janeiro: Livraria São José.

Dietrich, Wolf. 1990. More evidence for an internal classification of Tupi-Guarani languages. Indiana:12. Berlin: Gebr. Mann Verlag.

Dixon, R. M. W. 1994. Ergativity. Cambridge: Cambridge University Press.

Dobson, Rose. M. 1988. Aspectos da língua Kayabí. Série Linguística:12. Brasilia: Summer Institute of Linguistics.

Dooley, Robert A. 1982. Vocabulário do Guaraní. Brasilia: Summer Institute of Linguistics.

_______. 1991. A double-verb construction in Mbyá Guaraní. Work papers of the Summer Institute of Linguistics 35: 31-66.

_______. 1992. When switch reference moves to discourse: Developmental markers in Mbyá Guaraní. Language in Context: Essays for Robert E. Longacre, eds. Shin Ja J. Hwang and William R. Merrifield, pp. 97-108. Dallas: Summer Institute of Linguistics and University of Texas at Arlington Publications in Linguistics 107.

Harrison, Carl. 1986. Verb prominence, verb initialness, ergativity and typological disharmony in Guajajara. Handbook of Amazonian Languages. Vol. 1, eds. Desmond C. Derbyshire and Geoffrey K. Pullum, pp. 407-439. Berlin: Mouton de Gruyter.

Jensen, Cheryl. 1987. Object-prefix incorporation in Proto-Tupí-Guaraní Verbs. Language Sciences 9, No. 1:45-55.

_______. 1989. O desenvolvimento histórico da língua Wayampi. Campinas: Editora da UNICAMP.

_______. 1990. Cross-referencing changes in some Tupí-Guaraní languages. Amazonian Linguistics: Studies in Lowland South American Languages, ed. Doris L. Payne, pp. 117-158. Austin: University of Texas Press.

_______. 1998. Comparative Tupí-Guaraní morphosyntax. Handbook of Amazonian Languages, Vol. 4, eds. Desmond Derbyshire and Geoffrey Pullum. Berlin: Mouton de Gruyter.

Kakumasu, James. 1986. Urubu-Kaapor. Handbook of Amazonian Languages, Vol. 1, eds. Derbyshire and Pullum, 326-403. Berlin: Mouton de Gruyter.

Leite, Yonne. 1987. Referential hierarchy and Tapirapé split marking systems. MS presented at the Working Conference on Amazonian Languages, University of Oregon.

Newton, Dennis. 1978. Guarayu discourse. Work Papers of the Summer Institute of Linguistics. Riberalta: Summer Institute of Linguistics.

Nicholson, Velda. 1975. Initiating and non-initiating verbs in Assurini. Brasilia: Archives of the Summer Institute of Linguistics. MS.

Nicholson, Velda. 1978. Aspectos da língua Assuriní. Brasilia: Summer Institute of Linguistics.

Rodrigues, Aryon Dall'Igna. 1952. Análise morfológica de um texto Tupí. Curitiba: Logos, VII:15.

Rodrigues, Aryon Dall'Igna. 1953. Morfologia do verbo Tupí. Curitiba: Letras, No. 1.

Rodrigues, Aryon Dall'Igna. 1984/1985. Relações internas na família linguística Tupi-Guarani. Revista de Antropologia 27/28:33-53. São Paulo.

Rodrigues, Aryon D. 1985. Evidence for Tupi-Carib Relationships. South American Indian Languages: Retrospect and Prospect, ed. by Harriet E. Manelis Klein and Louisa R. Stark, pp. 371-404. Austin: University of Texas Press.

Rodrigues, Daniele M. G. 1997. Ergatividade em Guaraní Antigo: sistemas pessoal e relacional. MS presented at the Seminario permanente de línguas indígenas Amazônicas, Universidade Federal do Pará (Brazil.

Seki, Lucy. 1983. Observações sobre variação sociolinguística em Kamaiurá. Cadernos de Estudos Linguísticos, Vol. 4:73-87.

Seki, Lucy. 1989. Sistema de marcação de caso do Kamaiurá. MS presented at the Seminário de Tipologia. UNICAMP.

Seki, Lucy. 1990. Kamaiurá (Tupí-Guaraní) as an active-stative language. Amazonian Linguistics: Studies in Lowland South American Languages, ed. by Doris L. Payne, pp. 367-391. Austin: University of Texas Press.

Wiesemann, Ursula. 1986. Grammaticalized coreference. Pronominal Systems, ed. by U. Wiesemann, pp. 437-481. Tübingen: Gunter Narr Verlag.

Aspects of ergativity in Marubo (Panoan)

Raquel Guimarães Romankevicius Costa

Museu Nacional/UFRJ

1. Introduction

The purpose of this article is to provide an overview of various aspects of ergativity in Marubo, a Panoan language spoken by groups that live at Vale do Javari, a region that is located at the extreme west of the Brazilian state of Amazonas.[1] The analysis is based on a typological approach, in particular the model of ergativity proposed by Dixon (1994).

With this model in mind, we observe simple sentences, focusing our attention on the cases of split ergativity that arise in the language, especially those conditioned by the semantic nature of the verb and by the tense, aspect and modality system. We will show that in the former case the language operates according to the split-S system and, in the latter, the nominative-accusative pattern takes place.

Searching for syntactic motivations to classify the language as "syntactically ergative" or as "syntactically accusative", we examine some kinds of complex sentences, showing that in Marubo there are no syntactic constraints concerning either the combinations of certain types of sentences or the omission of coreferential constituents in coordinate and subordinate sen-

---

[1] Marubo speakers live at the headwaters of Ituí and Curuçá rivers, affluents of the left edge of Javari river, located at Vale do Javari, Alto Solimões region, at the extreme west of Amazonas state, next to the frontier between Brazil and Peru. According to an ethnographic study by Cavuscens and Neves (1986), the Marubo population comprised a total of 594 speakers at that time. Considering population increase indexes (based on data registered among 1963 and 1990), the actual population is about one thousand speakers. The study of the language has been executed since 1988, with speakers of São Sebastião settlement, in the mid Curuçá river. Two field studies have been made since then. The first contact took place from September to November 1988. A total of nine hours of recorded speech consisting of two questionnaires was made with just one informant. The second contact was made from April to June 1990, this time with two main informants, besides other recordings including the speech of children, women and other important persons in the community. About twenty hours of recording were made on this occasion, including six more questionnaires, stories, rituals and conversations. In respect to the language documentation, there has been no linguistic study of Marubo, except for a standard form containing only 163 items, filled up by Philip Ernest Boutle, a member of SIL, in 1964. See references for some recent works on Marubo syntax, morphology and phonology.

[JAL, vol. 1, no.2, March 1998, pp. 50-103]

tences. These facts will lead to the conclusion that Marubo can not be classified either as syntactically ergative or as syntactically accusative, the ergativity being manifested only at the morphological level.

In what follows we provide a sketch of Dixon's theory and then we go on with the analysis of Marubo.

2. Dixon's account of ergativity: S, A and O as universal syntactic-semantic primitives

The term *ergativity* is traditionally used to refer to a case-marking system—the *ergative-absolutive* system—which is characterized by the obedience to the transitivity of a sentence. Every language distinguishes intransitive, with a predicate and a singular core argument, from transitive sentences, with a predicate and two or more core arguments. According to Dixon (1994: 6), every language functions in terms of three universal syntactic-semantic primitives: **S**—subject of the intransitive sentence; **A**—subject of the transitive sentence; and **O**—direct object of the transitive sentence. The semantic basis for the establishment of these three syntactic basic relations is associated with the prototypical meaning of verbs. Prototypically, the semantic role of Agent, the most relevant participant for the success of an activity, is identified with A; the semantic role of Patient, the participant most saliently affected by the activity, is identified with O. Therefore, in a transitive sentence, A is differentiated from O. Such a distinction can be made in terms of word order, morphological case-marking, agreement or pronominal case-marking on the verb, the use of particles or clitics, or through the combination of different coding devices, including intonation (see also Givón 1984:146). On the other hand, in an intransitive sentence, the single participant will always be identified as S, regardless of the meaning of the verb or the semantic role assigned by it. It can be the Agent controller of the activity or the Patient affected by the activity. Thus, depending on the semantic type of verb, S can be identified now with A, now with O: it will be $\mathbf{S_a}$ if it is semantically similar to A; or $\mathbf{S_o}$ if it is semantically similar to O. S may then be marked like A, or like O, or differently from A and O. We conclude that the three basic grammatical relations—S, A and O—may be grouped in various ways, resulting in different mechanisms to indicate the syntactic function of S, A or O, as well as semantic contrasts between them.

It is well known that in an ergative-absolutive system S and O are identified by the same morphological marking, as opposed to A, with a distinct one. S and O are marked by the *absolutive* case. A is marked by the *ergative* case. Most commonly the ergative case presents an explicit morphological marking, while the unmarked case, absolutive, almost always has zero realization (ø).

As we will show in Section 3.1, this is exactly what happens in Marubo, an ergative Panoan language. The phenomenon of ergativity is also manifested in a number of other Brazilian indigenous languages such as those of the Carib family (cf. Franchetto, Vieira and Leite, Ms.), or those of the Tupí-Guaraní, Jê and Arawak families.

In typological studies, the ergative-absolutive system is seen as complementary to the *nominative-accusative* system (cf. Dixon 1994:1). In the latter, S and A receive the same treatment, being marked by the *nominative* case, as opposed to O, marked by the *accusative*. The nominative generally has zero realization, while the accusative is explicitly marked. Many languages combine both systems, resulting in various types of splits, which turn out to be conditioned by the semantic nature of the verb, by the semantic nature of NPs arguments, by the tense, aspect and modality system of the sentence, or by the grammatical status of the sentence (main versus subordinate clauses). These phenomena will be treated in detail in the body of the paper. In Section 3.2.2, for example, we will show that in the case of splits conditioned by tense, aspect and modality, Marubo functions according to the accusative pattern.

As noted by Dixon (1994:70-71), if the split is conditioned by the semantic nature of the verb, the result is a case-marking system with two subtypes of S: S_a with active verbs, and S_o with stative verbs, whereby S_a is marked like A and S_o is marked like O. Two systems arise as a consequence of this kind of split: the *split-S* system and the *fluid-S* system.

The split-S system, like the ergative and nominative systems, has a syntactically based marking (or prototypical marking). Each verb has a prototypical meaning and its arguments are marked grammatically according to their semantic function in the prototypical scheme, even when the verb is used with a non-prototypical meaning. Intransitive verbs are subdivided into two sets, nearly on semantic grounds, but each verb belongs to a fixed class —either S_a or S_o—generally based on its prototypical meaning (cf. Dixon 1994: 71-72). As an example of a split-S language, Dixon cites, among others, Mandan, from the Siouan family (cf. Kennard 1936, *apud* Dixon 1994). This kind of case-marking system is also found in languages of the Tupí-Guaraní family, as is the case of Kamayurá and Tapirapé (cf. Leite 1990), both spoken in Brazil. As will be demonstrated in 3.2.1, this case-marking pattern is also observed in Marubo.

The fluid-S system, on the other hand, employs syntactically based marking for transitive verbs (A and O are marked in accordance with the prototypical meaning of the verb) but semantically based marking (or direct marking) for intransitive verbs. S is marked according to its specific semantic function, in a specific situation of usage of the verb. Thus, the subject of an intransitive verb can be marked sometimes as S_a, sometimes as S_o. Each intransitive verb has in fact two possibilities of marking: S_a, when the referent of the S NP controls the activity; S_o, if there is no control. In practice, some verbs express activities that are always likely to be controlled and are always likely to be marked as S_a; others express activities or states that are likely never to be controlled and are always likely marked as S_o. Nevertheless, there is a variety of verbs that refer to activities that may or may not be controlled. These verbs admit either S_a or S_o marking, depending on the existence or lack of control (cf. Dixon, 1994: 78-79). An example of a fluid-S language cited by Dixon is Tsova-Tush, a Caucasian language (cf. Holysky, 1987, *apud* Dixon, 1994). He points out that at least one language spoken in Brazil—Baniwa do Içana, from the Arawak family—shows fluid-S characteristics.

In summary, Dixon (1994) proposes that while the split-S system operates with syntactic rules related to the prototypical scheme, the fluid-S system, regarding intransitive verbs, operates with semantic rules that directly describe the semantics of each situation of usage of the verb in question.

In conclusion, if we have, on one side, the identification of S and O, as opposed to A, in an ergative system, we have, on the other, the identification of S and A, as opposed to O, in a nominative system. Further, as a result of the splits between them, S_a and A are opposed to S_o and O in split-S and fluid-S systems.

In the following section we describe Marubo regarding the ergative case-marking devices used by the language. The subsequent sections are dedicated to our main purpose in this article—the analysis of the various kinds of manifestations of split ergativity in Marubo, together with a typological classification of the language along the lines proposed by the typological approach. The most important conclusions reached in the analysis are summed up in Section 5. An appendix with phonological information, including metrical constituents, is added at the end of the paper.

3. Morphological ergativity

3.1. Case-marking in Marubo

Case-marking in Marubo is of the ergative-absolutive type. The manifestation of ergativity in Marubo can be observed in the following examples:[2]

Transitive sentences

---

[2] According to our purpose of relating phonology to other linguistic levels (following Soares 1990, 1992), we work with phonetically represented data (cf. IPA symbols) because we feel that this relation can only be captured if we take all the details of the phonetic transcription in account. Since some phonological facts will be shown in the text as interconnected with ergativity, we add a phonemic line under the phonetic one. For information about phonological processes, metrical constituents and basic prominence assignment, the relation between nasalization and stress, as well as syllabification/resyllabification, see the Appendix, where a list of abbreviations is also found. On glosses referring to tense and aspect marking, see Section 3.2.2.

(01) a. vă'kɯ̃ 'ʔĩsɯ̆ 'yẽmămă'kātsĕɩ
va'kɨ-n 'isu-ø 'yamama-'katsai
child-ERG monkey-ABS kill-FUT
'The boy will kill the monkey.'

b. mă'nĩʃĭnĩ yŭ'ā 'tūʃăɩ
ma'niʃi-**nin** yu'a-ø 'tuʃa-ai
PN-ERG pan-ABS break-PRES/IM.PAST
'ma'niʃi has broken the pan.'

Intransitive sentences

(02) a. 'vākɯ̆ nŭ'kūăɩ
'vakɨ-ø nu'ku-ai
child-ABS arrive-PRES/IM.PAST
'The boy has arrived.'

b. mă'nĩʃĩ pă'kɯ̄ăɩ
ma'niʃi-ø pa'kɨ-ai
PN-ABS fall-PRES/IM.PAST
'ma'niʃi has fallen down.'

From the examples above we see that the absolutive case is not morphologically marked, that is, it is ø. The ergative case shows different morphological marks, depending on the morphological characterization of the NP with the ergativity marker. In (01 a), the ergative case is marked through syllabic prominence inversion, in conjunction with the nasalization of the last syllable of the noun. In (01 b) it is marked by the suffix **-nin**. According to Costa (1992), there are other ergative markers, which are subsumed below.

3.1.1. Ergative case in nominals

There are two types of case-marking in Marubo, which we named *type (a)* and *type (b)* (cf. Costa 1992: 97-108).

Type (a): nasalization

This consists of the noun's final vowel nasalization. Vowel nasalization is interpreted as the phonetic realization of the ergative morpheme [n], which closes the noun final syllable when it is affixed to it, thus propitiating the vowel nasalization. Along with nasalization, changes in syllabic prominence[3] may occur. Lexical stress in Marubo is characterized by maximal pitch, duration and intensity, the main correlate of which is pitch (duration and intensity are predicted from pitch). It is worth emphasizing that the stress shifts associated with ergative case-marking are not found in other suffixation processes, although alternating stress patterns in some verbal roots distinguish between transitive and intransitive usage. On the other hand, vowel nasalisation, combined with vowel changes associated with it, is better seen as a general phonological process in the language, which is conditioned by vowel contact with an immediately following nasal consonant (for more on nasalization, see Appendix).

This type of case-marking is found in monosyllables, in first syllable stressed disyllables and in simple or complex trisyllables.

---

[3] According to metrical theory, stress is the linguistic manifestation of rhythmic structure. Stress is seen as a hierarchically organized rhythmic structure, in the sense that it involves multiple levels or an indeterminate number of degrees. As first proposed by Liberman and Prince (1977), prominence relations must be accounted for in stress assignment. This relational aspect of stress is represented either through a metrical tree (derived from the syntactic tree) or to a metrical grid (derived from the metrical tree). The nodes of the tree are labeled S(trong) and W(eak) to mark relative prominence among constituents; and the metrical grid serves as a rhythmic interpretation of the tree, since it reflects successive levels of prominence, as well as the relative force of each constituent. According to Halle and Vergnaud (1987: 9), who adopt a model of bracketed metrical grid, "each stress domain contains exactly one rhythmic position that is distinguished from all others as being more prominent." As pointed out by Hayes (1991:22), who assumes a similar version of metrical theory, relative degrees of stress on the syllables are reflected in the grid column heights, while sequences of rhythmic beats on a particular level are represented in the grid rows. Since in the perspective of metrical theory stress is assumed as a matter of relative prominence and not absolute values, and since we are interested not only in stress but also in general rhythmic patterns in Marubo (cf. Appendix), we use both the terms "stress" and "syllabic prominence" throughout the paper.

We will thus refer to lexical and phrasal stress by the term "prominence." Both kinds of stress in Marubo have high pitch as their main correlate, which may be combined with long duration and high intensity. As for the term prominence, our preference for its use, instead of stress, is due to the results achieved by Nespor and Vogel (1989), in examining the possibilities of Beat Insertion manifestations in languages with stress systems and in languages with pitch systems (as manifestation of stress). They found clues in favor of an abstract notion of "prominence," which is neuter and seems to operate in both systems (cf. Nespor and Vogel 1989: 93, *apud* Soares, to appear). "Prominence" is then meant here as a general term for stress whatever phonetic means it is achieved by.

Monosyllabic nouns

As monosyllabic nouns always carry stress, case-marking is achieved just by means of final vowel nasalization resulting from the attachment of the ergative morpheme **-n**. As examples we have:

(03) ˈvō ˈvũ̄ ˈkɯ̃̄ⁿdă nĩˈkẽ̄ĩ
ˈvu ˈvu-**n** ˈkɯna-ø ninˈkan-ai
'proper noun' PN-ERG PN-ABS hear-PRES/IM.PAS
'ˈvu has heard ˈkɯna.'

Disyllabic nouns

Disyllables, in their great majority, are stressed in the first syllable. Besides final vowel nasalization, there is a simultaneous transference of the syllabic prominence of the first syllable to the second one, as can be seen in:[4]

(04) ˈkāmă kăˈmẽ̄ ˈkɯ̃̄pɯ̆ ˈkɯ̃̄nɯ̆ăvăɩ
ˈkama kaˈma-**n** ˈkɨnpu-ø ˈkɨnɨ-a-vai
'proper noun' PN-ERG pot-ABS paint-AUX(T)-REC.PAST
'ˈkama has painted the pot.'

Trissyllabic nouns

Simple or derived trisyllables, stressed in first or second syllable, are case marked just by final vowel nasalization. Syllabic prominence does not alter, no matter which syllable is stressed, as is seen in the following examples:[5]

(05) ˈtākăɾɨ̆ ˈtākăɾɯ̃ ˈwākăpăʃă ˈākă
ˈtakarɨ ˈtakarɨ-**n** ˈwakapaʃa-ø ˈa-ka
'chicken' chicken-ERG water-ABS AUX(T)-PRES/IM.PAST (= drink)
'The chicken(s) is/are drinking water.'

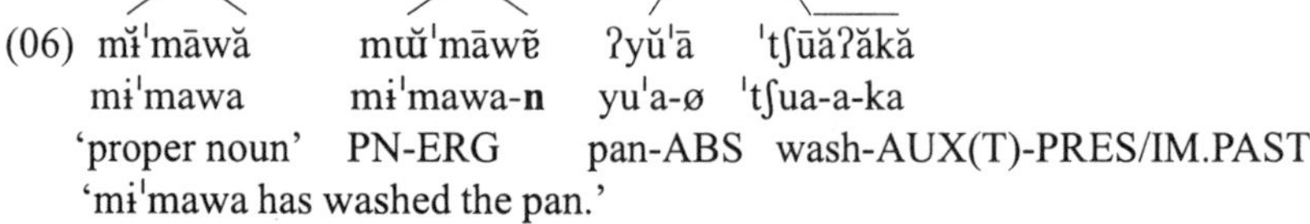

(06) mɨ̆ˈmāwă mɯ̆ˈmāwẽ ʔyŭˈā ˈtʃūăʔăkă
mɨˈmawa mɨˈmawa-**n** yuˈa-ø ˈtʃua-a-ka
'proper noun' PN-ERG pan-ABS wash-AUX(T)-PRES/IM.PAST
'mɨˈmawa has washed the pan.'

---

[4] In Dorigo and Costa (1996b), we established syllabic trochees as basic metrical feet for Marubo, constructed from left to right, with End Rule left (cf. Hayes 1991). See the Appendix for more information.

[5] Nasalized vowels that are not marked for duration in phonetic transcription (as in 05-07) are always short. They are not marked as such due to a failure in our IPA fonts tab.

Nevertheless, instead of nasalization, a new syllable may appear as an ergative case marker. This new syllable consists of a nasal consonant plus a high vowel, which is harmonized with the preceding vowel, in respect to local constriction. In (07), the high vowel added to the nasal [n], harmonizes to the preceding vowel [i], in that both are coronal.[6] In this case, the new syllable vowel nasality is conditioned by the final nasal consonant. The /nVn/ morpheme is then phonetically realized as [**nĩ**].

(07) mă'nīʃĩ mă'nīʃinĩ ẽ'ātsă 'nīsă
ma'niʃi ma'niʃi-**nin** an-'atsa-ø 'nisa-a
'proper noun' PN-ERG 3A-SG-cassava-ABS rasp-PRES/IM.PAST
'ma'niʃi is rasping the cassava.'

Type (b): suffixation

Ergative case-marking of this type is characterized by the addition of a monosyllabic case-marking suffix, whose forms vary according to the morphological characteristics of the noun or noun phrase to which it is attached. Syllabic prominence changes may also occur.

Type (b) marking is found in last syllable stressed disyllables, also involving syllabic prominence changes. It is also found in compound nouns and in complex noun phrases, but with no changes in syllabic prominence.

Disyllabic nouns

In disyllables with stress on the last syllable, the suffix **-pa** is added. Simultaneously, the stress in the last syllable is transferred to the first one, as seen in (08).

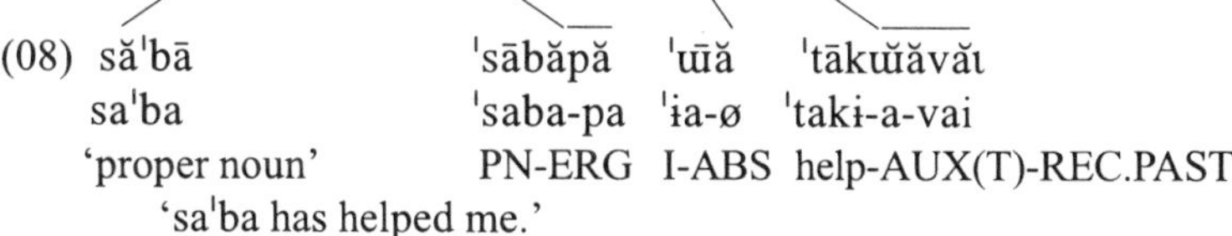

(08) să'bā 'sābăpă 'ɯ̃ă 'tākɯ̃ăvăɩ
sa'ba 'saba-pa 'ɨa-ø 'takɨ-a-vai
'proper noun' PN-ERG I-ABS help-AUX(T)-REC.PAST
'sa'ba has helped me.'

In disyllables of the same type, but with final vowel bearing nasality (that is, when the last syllable is closed by a nasal consonant), the ergative case-marking yields the rising of a new syllable, consisting of a nasal consonant plus a high vowel, which harmonizes, in articulatory terms, to the preceding vowel. This can be observed in (09), where the high vowel of the new syllable shares the feature [dorsal] with the preceding vowel /a/. Simultaneously, the last syllable prominence of the noun is transferred to the first one.

[6] In respect to point of articulation and stricture degree, we assume —like Clements and Hume (1995) —that the same set of features is required for consonants and vowels in a feature system (see the Appendix).

(09) kă'mẽ̄ 'kẽ̄mẽ̄nɯ̆̃ 'wākăpăʃă 'ākă
ka'man 'kama-nɨ 'wakapaʃa-ø 'a-ka
'jaguar' jaguar-ERG water-ABS AUX(T)-PRES/IM.PAST (= drink)
'The jaguar is drinking water.'

Compound nouns and complex NPs

Compound nouns, formed through OV structure (cf. Costa 1992: 56), are marked by the nasalized suffix **-tun**, with no syllabic prominence changes, as seen in the example below:

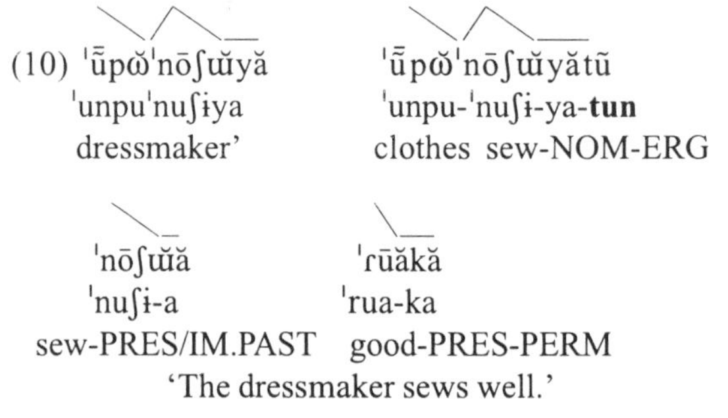
(10) 'ũ̄pɯ̆̃'nōʃɯ̆̃yă 'ũ̄pɯ̆̃'nōʃɯ̆̃yătũ
'unpu'nuʃɨya 'unpu-'nuʃɨ-ya-**tun**
dressmaker' clothes sew-NOM-ERG

'nōʃɯ̆̃ă 'ɾūăkă
'nuʃɨ-a 'rua-ka
sew-PRES/IM.PAST good-PRES-PERM
'The dressmaker sews well.'

In complex noun phrases, the same suffix marks the whole construction, which may show changes in syllabic prominence, according to a rhythmic pattern rule operation:[7]

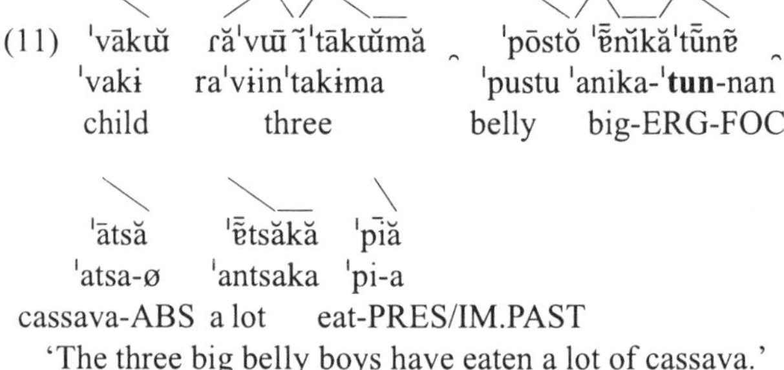
(11) 'vākɯ̆ ɾă'vɯ̄ ĩ'tākɯ̆mă 'pōstŏ 'ẽ̄nĭkă'tũ̄nẽ̄
'vakɨ ra'vɨin'takɨma 'pustu 'anika-'**tun**-nan
child three belly big-ERG-FOC

'ātsă 'ẽ̄tsăkă 'pīă
'atsa-ø 'antsaka 'pi-a
cassava-ABS a lot eat-PRES/IM.PAST
'The three big belly boys have eaten a lot of cassava.'

From the data observed above, we conclude that Marubo makes use of combinations among (a) nasalization and stress; (b) morphology and stress;

[7] There is in Marubo a rhythmic pattern rule, which establishes that "the maximum limit of non-prominent syllables in a noun (and in a complex NP) is only three" (cf. Costa 1992:44). In order that this limit be respected in (11), the suffix **-tun** acquires prominence, when the discursive marker **-nan** is added, so that general rhythmic patterns can be reestablished, that is, to avoid violation of the referred rhythmic rule. For another approach to rhythmic regulation rules see the Appendix (level 2 stress assignment).

(c) morphology and nasalization; and, in certain cases, (d) only nasalization, as ergative case-marking devices.[8]

3.1.2. Ergative case in pronominals

According to Costa (1996 a), the personal pronominal system, as generally, has as starting point the speaker-addressee axis. There are free forms for reference of the speaker to himself (singular first person): **ˈɨa**; and for reference of the speaker to the addressee (singular second person): **ˈmia**; for reference to speaker and someone else (plural first person, without the distinction inclusion/exclusion): **ˈnukɨ**; and for reference of the speaker to more than one addressee, or the addressee and someone else (plural second person): **ˈmatu**.

Persons or entities out of the speaker-addressee axis, that is, third person forms, have as source the demonstratives, whose reference point is the speaker's place position—proximity, distance and visibility. The form **ˈna** is used to refer to "what is proximal and visible to the speaker (*this*);" **ˈwa**, to "what is distant and visible to the speaker (*that*);" and **ˈa** to "what is distant and out of the speaker's field of vision (*that*)." The notion of visibility may extend to the addressee since he may be inside the speaker's field of vision.

The singular third person form **ˈwa**, without gender distinction and still with deictic meaning, has thus gestural usage. Besides **ˈwa**, the form **ˈa** has symbolic usage to refer to a person or entity out of the speaker's field of vision. It is also used to refer to a previous indication, in anaphoric usage. In other words, besides symbolic usage, **ˈa** represents an element about whom one is talking, thus referring to the same entity referred to by a term already mentioned, explicitly or implicitly, in the linguistic context. On the other hand, **ˈwa** codes the element referred to by the speaker at the moment of communication (*that element I see there*).

The same forms, added by the formative **-rasin**, are used in the plural, for masculine and feminine: **ˈwarasin** and **ˈarasin**. Other variations are the forms **ˈatu** and **ˈatuvu**, with symbolic and anaphoric usage. The last one is added by the formative **-vu**, which indicates indefinite plural or generalization of a class or group of elements defined as a set (as in ***ˈyuinivu***, *all the animals*).

---

[8] It is worth observing that the same devices used to mark ergative case are also used to mark locative (cf. 53), instrumental (cf. 56), means and genitive-possessive cases (cf. Costa 1992). As we consider the hypothesis assumed in Costa (1993), we cannot separate morphological case from positional licensing ("abstract Case") in Marubo. According to that hypothesis, "the syntactic representation bears the existence of an external argument, which, necessarily marked by morphology, is opposed to internal arguments, which, being assigned structural case, dispense with morphological marking" (see footnotes 9 and 17). We are thus interpreting Marubo case-marking as ergative and not "quirky case," as defined by Levin and Simpson (1981) (*apud* Schütze 1993). This subject will be better explored in future research on Marubo.

The same devices for marking the ergative case in nominal forms are also used for pronominal forms (cf. Costa 1992:108-115), as can be observed in Table 1 below, which shows the personal pronouns system of Marubo, in free forms, in the absolutive and ergative cases.

	Singular		Plural	
	absolutive	*ergative*	*absolutive*	*ergative*
1st person	'ɯ̄ă 'ɨa	ɯ̆'ẽ̄ ɨ'a-n	'nūkɯ̆ 'nukɨ	nŭ'kɯ̃̄ nu'kɨ-n
2nd person	'mīă 'mia	mĭ'ẽ̄ mi'a-n	'mātŏ 'matu	mă'tũ̄ ma'tu-n
3rd person	'a 'a	'ẽ̄tũ 'an-tun	'āɾăsĩ̄ 'a-rasin	'āɾăsĩ̄ni 'a-rasi-ni
symbolic and	–	–	'ātŏ 'atu	–
anaphoric usage	–	–	'ātŏvŏ 'atu-vu	'ātŏvũ 'atu-vu-n
3rd person gestural usage	'wā 'wa	'wẽ̄tũ 'wan-tun	'wāɾăsĩ̄ 'wa-rasin	'wāɾăsĩ̄nĭ 'wa-rasin-ni

Table 1: Personal pronouns

The ergative case-marking for singular and plural first and second persons is of the **(a)** type, as can be seen in Table 1. The following sentences show some of the forms in question, in absolutive and ergative cases:

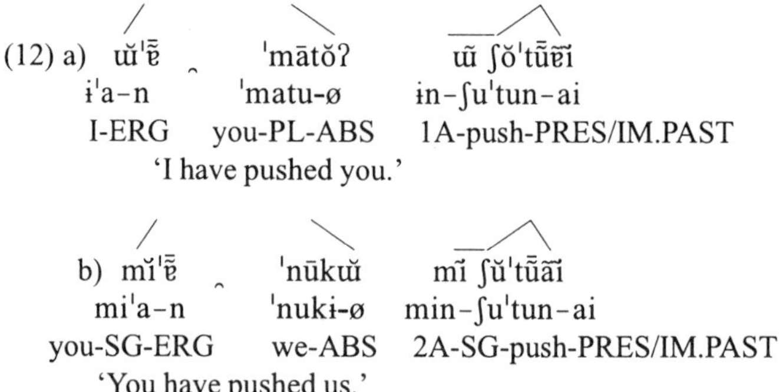

(12) a) ɯ̆'ẽ̄ 'mātŏ? ɯ̃ ʃŏ'tũ̄ẽ̄ĩ
ɨ'a-n 'matu-ø ɨn-ʃu'tun-ai
I-ERG you-PL-ABS 1A-push-PRES/IM.PAST
'I have pushed you.'

b) mĭ'ẽ̄ 'nūkɯ̆ mĩ ʃŭ'tũ̄ãĩ
mi'a-n 'nukɨ-ø min-ʃu'tun-ai
you-SG-ERG we-ABS 2A-SG-push-PRES/IM.PAST
'You have pushed us.'

c) nŭˈkɯ̃ĩ ‿ ˈmīă nũ ʃŭˈtũɐ̃ĩ
nuˈkɨ-n ˈmia-ø nun-ʃuˈtun-ai
we-ERG you-SG-ABS 1A-PL-push-PRES/IM.PAST
'We have pushed you.'

d) măˈtũ ‿ ˈɯ̃ă mɐ̃ ʃŭˈtũãĩ
maˈtu-n ˈɨa-ø man-ʃuˈtun-ai
you-PL-ERG I-ABS 2A-PL-push-PRES/IM.PAST
'You have pushed us.'

The ergative case-marking for third person singular is of the **(b)** type, with the addition of the nasalized formative **-tun** to the absolutive base. The nasality of this suffix is assimilated by the final low vowel of the base, which is then raised. In the plural both types occur. The formative **-ni** is added to trisyllabic bases ended with nasalized high front vowel, with no syllabic prominence alterations. The trisyllabic base ended with high back vowel is only nasalized. The form **ˈatu** is used only in absolutive case, as direct object. The transitive sentences below show some occurrences of these forms.

(13) a. ˈɐ̃tũ ‿ ˈā ‿ ʃŭˈtũɐ̃ĩ
ˈan-tun ˈa-ø ʃuˈtun-ai
(s)he-ERG (s)he-ABS push-PRES/IM.PAST
'He/she has pushed him/her.'

b. ˈwɐ̃tũ ‿ ˈwā ‿ ʃŭˈtũɐ̃ĩ
ˈwan-tun ˈwa-ø ʃuˈtun-ai
(s)he-ERG (s)he-ABS push-PRES/IM.PAST
He/she (that one) has pushed him/her.'

c. ˈɐ̃tũ ‿ ˈārăsĩ ‿ ʃŭˈtũɐ̃ĩ
ˈan-tun ˈa-rasin-ø ʃuˈtun-ai
(s)he-ERG (s)he-PL-ABS push-PRES/IM.PAST
'He/she has pushed them.'

d. ˈārăsĩnĩ ‿ ˈātɷ̆ ‿ ʃŭˈtũɐ̃ĩ
ˈa-rasin-ni ˈatu-ø ʃuˈtun-ai
(s)he-PL-ERG they-ABS push-PRES/IM.PAST
'He/she has pushed them.'

e. ˈā tŏvũ ˈātῶvῶ ʃŭˈtũ̄ɐ̃ĩ
ˈatu-vu-n ˈatu-vu-ø ʃuˈtun-ai
(s)he-PL-ERG (s)he-PL-ABS push-PRES/IM.PAST
'They have pushed him/her.'

f. ˈwāɾ̆ĭsĩnĭ ˈwāɾ̆ĭsĩ ʃŭˈtũ̄ɐ̃ĩ
ˈwa-rasin-ni ˈwa-rasin-ø ʃuˈtun-ai
(s)he-PL-ERG (s)he-PL-ABS push-PRES/IM.PAST
'They have pushed them.'

3.1.3. Agentivity and transitivity

Comrie (1978:356) rejects the identification of ergativity and agentivity, arguing that, despite some similarities between both, there is evidence from a wide range of ergative languages that points against this identification. He points out that the main kind of evidence concerns verbs that are basically transitive, that is, verbs that normally take a direct object, but which can be used also without an object, although the same interpretation of agentivity is present in both. In some ergative languages, as in Basque, the subject of such an objectless transitive verb remains in the ergative case. These languages provide some evidence of a link between ergativity and agentivity. In many other ergative languages, however, the subject of such verbs stands in the absolutive case, as is the case of Tongan. Depending on the language, a marker is also required on the verb in such constructions to indicate that it is being used intransitively, as in Dyirbal. These facts provide evidence that the ergative marking is sensitive to the transitivity of the verb, thus implying consequences in syntax. Another piece of evidence against the identification of ergativity and agentivity is that in many languages NPs marked with ergative case are not necessarily agentives. So, although there is a connection between ergativity and agentivity, the ergative marking does not necessarily involve a difference in degree of agentivity in the NP.

In Marubo, the subject of a basically transitive verb remains in the ergative case when the object is not expressed. Compare the examples below:

(14) ˈɐ̃̄tũ ˈpɐ̃̄nĭ ˈnɯ̄ʃăɩ
ˈan-tun ˈpani-ø ˈnɨʃa-ai
he-ERG net-ABS tear-PRES/IM.PAST
'He is tearing the net.'

(15) a. ˈẽ̄tũ ˈnɯ̃ʃăɩ b. * ˈā ˈnɯ̃ʃăɩ
ˈan-tu**n** ˈnɨʃa-ai ˈa-ø ˈnɨʃa-ai
he-ERG tear-PRES/IM.PAST he-ABS tear-PRES/IM.PAST
'He is tearing.' 'He is tearing.'

The constructions above show that ergativity is related to agentivity — the notion of agentivity is present in both the transitive and the intransitive. Other constructions in Marubo show the existence of the auxiliary verbs **a** and **i**, which occur respectively in transitive and intransitive constructions. These auxiliaries behave like light verbs, since they can have different meanings when they function as main verbs, depending on the context where they occur, as can be seen, for example, in (05) (cf. Costa 1992:77). The following are examples of the occurrence of these auxiliaries.

(16) ˈẽ̄tũ ˈpẽ̄nĭ tŏˈɾāʃăkă
ˈan-tu**n** ˈpani-ø toˈraʃ-**a**-ka
he-ERG net-ABS tear-AUX(T)-PRES/IM.PAST
'He has torn the net.'

(17) ˈpẽ̄nĭ tŏˈɾāʃikĭ
ˈpani-ø toˈraʃ-**i**-ki
net-ABS tear-AUX(I)-PRES/IM.PAST
'The net has torn.'

In Costa (1966b), forms like **toˈraʃ-a-ka** and **toˈraʃ-i-ki** are analyzed as resulting from the incorporation of an NP into a light verb. Thus, in addition to transitive or intransitive verbal roots, we also have in Marubo nominal roots that may be used transitively or intransitively. In the latter case, the subject will be marked with the ergative case, if the root is incorporated into **a**, and with the absolutive case, if it is incorporated into **i**. From (16) and (17) above we see that the ergative subject is the controller agent, and the absolutive subject is the patient affected by the verbal activity. The processes of transitivization and intrasitivization of nominal roots in Marubo show again the connection between ergativity and agentivity. The example below shows, however, that an ergative NP is not necessarily agentive.

(18) ŭˈī ˈvẽ̄năɾăsĩ mɯ̆ˈtʃāăkă
uˈi-**n** ˈvana-rasin-ø mɨˈtʃa-a-ka
rain-ERG plant-PL-ABS wet-AUX(T)-PRES/IM.PAST
'The rain has wet the plants.'

We see from this sentence that ergativity is related to the transitivity-intransitivity axis. Sensitive to transitivity, the ergative marking in (18) occurs for syntactic reasons and not for semantic ones.

As we have already observed, Dixon (1994) between languages that have syntactically based marking from languages with semantically based marking. In languages of the first type the arguments are marked grammatically, according to the prototypical meaning of the verb. The same marking remains, even if the verb is used with a non-prototypical meaning. In languages of the second type, the arguments are marked according to a specific function, in a specific situation of verb usage.

From (18) we see that Marubo shows a syntactically based marking. By metaphorical extension, non-agentive subjects of transitive verbs are marked the same way as the agent of a prototypical transitive construction. We conclude thus that, although the ergativity is closely related to agentivity in Marubo, there are also syntactic motivations for the ergative marking.

3.2. Split ergativity

3.2.1. Split conditioned by the semantic nature of the verb

Besides free-form pronominals, there are also person markers that precede nominal or verbal roots in Marubo. These are clitics that function as anaphoric pronouns, coreferentials with the subject free noun or pronoun. When they precede nouns, they may also take the function of possessives (see 21), if they are not coreferential with the subject (cf. Costa 1992: 208).[9]

These forms are monosyllables with no rhythmic autonomy, which result

[9] In Costa (1992:119-129), these forms were considered clitics (and not prefixes) based on certain criteria such as: (a) their occurrence in the face of free pronouns — both may occur at the same immediately pre-verbal position; both can be omitted, with no consequences to the grammaticality of the sentence; (b) their position in relation to the bounded forms in the language —they occur at the left of nominal or verbal roots, while bounded forms are positioned to the right; (c) their position of occurrence —immediately pre-verbal; before an object; before two objects. The possibilities of occurrence of these forms before two objects bring into question the hypothesis of object incorporation in Marubo, since the incorporation of more than one nominal root in a single verbal theme is generally impossible (cf. Mithun 1984). So these forms cliticize into verbs and nouns but they are not part of them. As clitics, these forms may take a grammatical status, since we can assume that they function as subject (for a proposal in which clitics may bear the status of arguments, see Jelinek 1984). This would lead us to question the syntactic position of what we have been calling "ergative subject," which in this case would be an adjunct. This would in turn explain the similarity between ergative and locative, instrumental, means and genitive-possessive case-marking.

from the contractions of free-form pronominals in the ergative case, as shown by the system below. Having no rhythmic autonomy (that is, they do not bear stress), these dependent pronominal forms cliticize most frequently to the left of the verbal form, but they may cliticize to the left of O, referring, in both positions, to the subject, be it S or A. The clitic's host is then always to its right, be it the verb or the object.[10]

	Singular	Plural
1	ɯ̃ ɨn	nũ nun
2	mĩ min	mẽ man
3	ẽ an	ătũ atun

Table 2: Pronominal clitics

These person markers appear both in transitive and in intransitive constructions. Therefore they are not related to the transitivity-intransitive axis. Below we show some occurrences of such forms (other occurrences can be seen in (12)).[11]

[10]According to Uriagereka (1995:83), although morphophonological and prosodic matters play a role in clitic placement, such factors are not the prime determinants of placement. Then an approach is needed that is sensitive to the syntactic/semantic shape of the clause in which the clitic is placed. From what has been observed above, we can add that pronominal clitics in Marubo are not second position clitics. Second position clitics would be sentential clitics, that is, clitics to which the debated "law" of Wackernagel would apply. According to this law, they would take, in some languages, the second position after the first stressed constituent (or word) of the sentence. Those clitics, meant as constituents of S, presuppose the modification of S, which is commonly achieved by means of the adverbialization or modalization of S (cf. Soares 1992, based on Kaisse 1982, 1985). This is not the case in Marubo since in this language clitic placement has nothing to do with sentence position, but with the host category, as can be seen from the relevant examples.

[11] The third person plural clitic is found, in rare cases, coreferential to the ergative subject, as seen in:

ˈwa-rasin-ni	ˈwa-ø	atun-ˈrua-a-ka
(s)he-PL-ERG	(s)he-ABS	3A-PL-like-AUX(T)-PRES/IM.PAST

'They like him/her.'

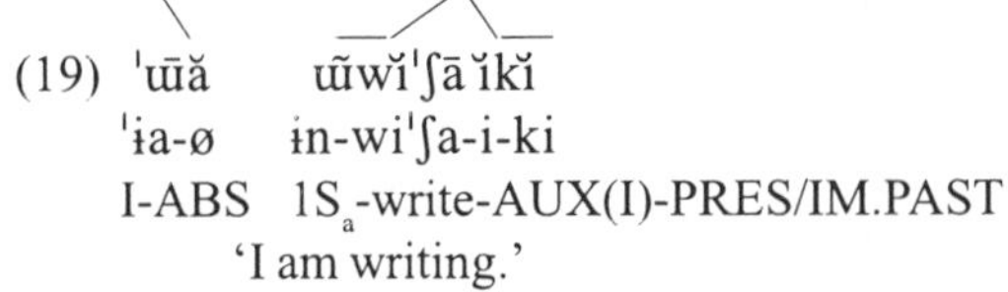

(19) ˈɯ̃ă ɯ̃wĭˈʃă ĭkĭ
ˈɨa-ø ɨn-wiˈʃa-i-ki
I-ABS 1S$_a$-write-AUX(I)-PRES/IM.PAST
'I am writing.'

(20) ˈmĩă ˈɾẽmăkăsɯ̆ mĩmŭˈnũăɩ
ˈmia-ø ˈramaka-sɨ min-muˈnu-ai
you-SG-ABS now-manner 2S$_a$-SG-dance-PRES/IM.PAST
'You are dancing now.'

(21) ˈtʃẽnŏ ẽˈɯ̃wănĩ ẽˈnĩă
ˈtʃano-ø **an**-ˈɯwa-nin **an**-ˈni-a
PN-ABS 3-POSS-mother-ASSOC 3S$_a$-SG-stay-PRES/IM.PAST
'ˈtʃano stays with his mother.'

(22) măˈtũ mɯ̆ˈẽ mẽˈtʃăʃĭĕɩ
maˈtu-n mɨˈan-ø **man**-ˈtʃaʃi-ai
you-PL-ERG branch-ABS 2A-PL-break-PRES/IM.PAST
'You have broken the branch.'

(23) ˈwẽtũ ẽˈpẽnĭ tŭˈɾăʃăkă
ˈwan-tun **an**-ˈpani-ø tuˈraʃ-a-ka
he-ERG 3A-SG-net-ABS tear-AUX(T)-PRES/IM.PAST
'He has torn the net.'

(24) ɯ̆ˈẽ ɯ̃kăˈmẽ ˈwĩẽɩ ˈnɯ̃nɯ̃mă
ɨˈan ɨn-kaˈman-ø ˈwin-ai ˈnɨnu-ma
I-ERG 1A-jaguar-ABS see-PRES/IM.PAST here-NEG
'I have seen jaguar far from here.'

The co-ocurrence of coreferent free-form (pro)nominals and pronominal clitics in the examples above seems to be what has been called in the literature as "clitic doubling". Among languages in which such a phenomenon was noted, we can cite Standard Spanish and River Plate Spanish (cf. Jaeggly, 1982), Porteño Spanish (cf. Suñer 1990), Welsh (cf. Sadler 1988), Pirahã (Everett 1987) and Yagua (cf. Everett (1989). As pointed out by Everett (1996: 46), not all languages with clitics allow clitic doubling, as is the case in standard French. But languages that do allow clitic doubling vary in respect to the kinds of restrictions imposed on the double, so that "Standard Spanish allows doubling of indirect objects, River Plate Spanish allows doubling of indirect objects and animate direct objects, Porteño Spanish allows doubling of any object, and all dialects of Spanish require doubling of pronouns." Pirahã, an Amazonian language from the Muran family, allows doubling of direct object, subject, possessor of NP, and object of postposition positions (Everett 1996:82). We can add that as long as the facts of Marubo presented above can be analyzed as clitic doubling, this language allows for doubling of subject.[12]

From the examples above we can see that the free-form nominals and pronominals are marked according to the ergative-absolutive system. A is marked by the ergative case. S and O receive the same marker ø of absolutive case. Nevertheless the pronominal clitics do not operate on the same basis. They are coreferential with S or A; and there is no pronominal clitic form for O. We see from these facts that Marubo is not a "consistently" [13] ergative language, since it operates with two systems —one for nominal case-marking and another for the cliticized pronouns.

We might suppose, from the data above, that the pronominal clitics would operate according to the nominative-accusative system, since they mark S an A, as opposed to O. A close inspection of the data reveals, nevertheless, that the occurrence of these clitics is semantically motivated —they occur with certain semantic types of verbs, depending on the semantic roles that they assign to their arguments. They case-mark the Agent or the Experiencer of transitive verbs and the Agent of intransitive active verbs. The Patient affected by the activity is not explicitly marked. These facts can be observed if we compare the examples in (19)-(24) with the following constructions:

---

[12] As we are considering the clitics in Marubo in terms of case-marking systems, we do not go further into the issue of clitic doubling here. For a minimalist account on the relationship between pronominal clitics and agreement affixes and pronouns, see Everett (1996). A minimalist approach on clitic placement in Western Romance can be seen in Uriagereka (1995).

[13] Warlpiri, a Pama-Nyangan Australian language, has an ergative-absolutive system for nominal case-marking and a nominative-accusative system for verb agreement (cf. Hale 1973). The same is true for Gahuku, a Papuan language, with a verbal prefix cross-referencing S and A and a verbal suffix cross-referencing O, while nouns are marked on an ergative-absolutive basis (cf. Deibler 1966). De Lancey (1985) points out that the confusion surrounding the classification of Tibetan, which he considers a typical representative of the active type, is due partly to the fact that "apparently among various dialects and various stages of the classical language, several different case-marking patterns occur, including active, aspectually split ergative, and consistent ergative, and minor variations of all three." Other inconsistencies regarding case-marking can be seen in Comrie (1978:340-344).

(25) ˈā̇ măˈvūpĭĕɩ
ˈa-ø ma-ˈvupi-ai
he-ABS already die-PRES/IM.PAST
'He has already died.'

(26) ˈā̇ ˈūʃăɩ
ˈa-ø ˈuʃa-ai
he-ABS sleep-PRES/IM.PAST
'He is sleeping.'

(27) ˈɾāvŭʃɯ̆ ĭˈʃīẽĩ
ˈravuʃɨ-ø iˈʃin-ai
knee-ABS ache-PRES/IM.PAST
'The knee is aching.'

(28) ˈɯ̄ă ɾăˈkāă
ˈɨa-ø raˈka-ai
I-ABS lie-PRES/IM.PAST
'I am lying.'

(29) ˈnūkɯ̆ ʃŭˈpīẽĩ
ˈnukɨ-ø ʃuˈpin-ai
we-ABS be hungry-PRES/IM.PAST
'We are hungry.'

(30) ˈmīă ĭʃˈnākă
ˈmīă-ø ĭʃˈnā-kă
you-ABS bad-PRES-PERM
'You are bad.'

(31) nă ˈvīmĭ ĭʃˈnāyă
na-ˈvi mi-ø iʃˈna-ya
DEM-fruit-ABS bad-PRES-RES
'This fruit is spoiled.'

(32) ăˈkū̃pă ˈvūpĭyă
a'kunpa-ø 'vupi-ya
PN-ABS die-PRES-RES
'a'kunpa is dead.'

As we consider these new data, we see that the language distinguishes verbs in the following ways: (a) active transitive verbs, like *drink*, *sew*, *rasp* and *wash*, including in this class verbs of cognition, like *think* , *see*, *hear*, *tell*, which require an Experiencer participant, and which, by metaphorical extension, are also considered active verbs; (b) active intransitive verbs indicating action, movement, or change in position, like *sing*, *cry*, *run*, *dance*, *fall*, *stand up*, *sit down*; (c) stative intransitive verbs, like *die*, *sleep*, *ache*, including here verbs that indicate body position, like *be sitting*, *be on foot, be lying*; feeling or sensation, like *be sad* , *be angry* , *be thirsty*; and adjectival forms that denote inherent quality or permanent state, or quality resulting from a change of state, like *be bad*, *become bad*, *be dead.*

Thus, case-marking in Marubo is also related to verb classes since it distinguishes two subtypes of S, according to the semantic nature of the verb: S_a for active intransitive verbs; and S_o, for intransitive stative verbs. S_a is semantically similar to A, in the sense that both exert control over the activity; S_o is semantically similar to O, in the sense that both are affected by the activity. Such a distinction is reflected through the pronominal clitics, in the form of a cross-reference system, which provides information about person and number of the NP in A or S_a function. On the other hand, there are no explicit forms for S_o. We conclude that, regarding pronominal clitics, Marubo is a split-S language since it operates in terms of an S category subdivided, with certain grammatical purposes, into S_a and S_o. It is a syntactically-based system since it always operates in the same way, irrespective of the semantics of a particular instance of use. Thus, an active (intransitive or transitive) verb can be preceded by a pronominal clitic, which is coreferential with either S_a or A, even if in a specific situation of verb usage S_a or A do not exert control over the activity. This can be observed in the examples below, where the presence or absence of control over the activity is expressed lexically, not through nominal case-marking or through pronominal clitics.

(33) ˈpūyă ˈāskăˈtāɪ ẽpăˈkɯ̄ɾĭvĭ
'puya-ø 'aska'tai an-pa'kɨ-rivi
PN-ABS on purpose 3S_a-SG-fall-EMPH
''puya has fallen on purpose.'

(34) ˈpūyă păˈkɯ̄nɐ̃ ăˈɾ̄i ɐ̃ĭˈk̄imă
ˈpuya-ø paˈkɨ-nan a-ˈri an-i-ˈki-ma
PN-ABS fall-FOC 3-REFL-SG 3S_a-SG-AUX(I)-PRES/IM.PAST-NEG
'ˈpuya has fallen; he did not do it by himself (by his fault).'

(35) măˈnīʃinĩ ˈākω̆ ˈpākɯ̆ˈvɐ̃̄nɐ̃
maˈniʃi-nin ˈaku-ø ˈpakɨ-ˈvan-nan
PN-ERG PN-ABS throw-MOV-FOC

ˈāskătăăˈkĩ̄ ɐ̃ăˈkā
ˈaskataaˈkin an-a-ˈka
on purpose 3S_a-SG-AUX(T)-PRES/IM.PAST
'maˈniʃi has thrown ˈaku down; she did it on purpose.'

(36) măˈnīʃinĩ ˈākω̆ ˈpākɯ̆ˈvɐ̃̄nɐ̃
maˈniʃi-nin ˈaku-ø ˈpakɨ-ˈvan-nan
PN-ERG PN-ABS throw-MOV-FOC

ăˈɾ̄i ɐ̃ăˈkāmă
a-ˈri an-a-ˈka-ma
3-REFL-SG 3S_a-SG-AUX(T)-PRES/IM.PAST-NEG
'maˈniʃi has thrown ˈaku down; she did not do it by herself (by her fault).'

Although some scholars consider the split-S system, also known as *active-inactive*, as an autonomous system for marking syntactic function, Dixon (1994:77) maintains that "split-S systems do involve a mixture of ergative and accusative patterns—S_a is marked like A and differently from O (the criterion for accusativity) while S_o is marked like O and differently from A (the criterion for ergativity)." In his view, there are two simple patterns of syntactic identification—accusative and ergative. And the Split-S system is no more than a split between those two basic systems. Resulting or not from a split between the ergative and accusative systems, the split-S system, which is manifested in Marubo through pronominal clitics, operates independently from the ergative system, which is manifested through nominal case-marking.

Despite being coreferentials with A and S_a, pronominal clitics are not interpreted as constituting an agreement system in Marubo in the face of the following facts:

(a) Their occurrence is not obligatory, as can be observed from the examples below (compare especially the pair 23-38).

(37) ˈvākɯ̆ nŭˈkūăɩ
ˈvakɨ-ø nuˈku-ai
child-ABS arrive-PRES/IM.PAST
'The boy has arrived.'

(38) ˈwẽ̄tũ ˈpẽ̄nĭ tŭˈɾāʃăkă
ˈwan-tun ˈpani-ø tuˈraʃ-a-ka
he-ERG net-ABS tear-AUX(T)-PRES/IM.PAST
'He has torn the net.'

(b) They occur in the same position as free-form (pro)nominals occur—before V or before O. Therefore, free-form (pro)nominals and pronominal clitics are interchangeable; both can be omitted (a fact which is well known in other languages).[14] And the presence of one or another is enough to identify A or S_a. Compare the examples above with the following ones:

(39) ˈɾẽ̄mă nũmŭˈnūkătsă
ˈrama nun-muˈnu-katsai
now $1S_a$-PL-dance-FUT
'Now we will dance.'

(40) ẽ̆ˈkẽ̄tĭ ˈkɯ̄wĭˈnẽ̄
an-ˈkanti-ø ˈkɨwi-ˈnan
$3S_a$-SG-bow-ABS stretch-FOC
'He is stretching the bow.'

The pronominal clitics thus constitute an independent system of syntactic marking. They cliticize to the left of V or to the left of O simply from phonological reasons, that is, because they bear no stress, these monosyllabic forms have no rhythmic autonomy (cf. Costa 1992:130).

We conclude then that Marubo shows two autonomous systems that allow for the establishment of grammatical relations: the (pro)nominal case-

[14] As pointed out by Dixon (1994:95), verbal cross-reference makes free-form pronouns in core functions virtually redundant so that they tend to occur less frequently, for purposes of emphasis. This is the case of modern Warlpiri, where free-form pronouns have a secondary role, being used only for emphasis. As noted by Comrie (1978:339), independent pronouns are normally omitted, unless stressed, in Quiché, a Mayan Language of Guatemala. In Gavião, (a language of the Mondé family, spoken in the Brazilian state of Rondônia), either an explicit NP or a pronominal prefix indicating person or number can be used to refer to core arguments (cf. Moore 1984, *apud* Dixon 1994:46). In respect to clitic doubling, it is worth noting the optionality and mobility of Spanish object clitics, as well as all kinds of doubling in Pirahã (cf. Everett 1996).

marking system, which operates according to the ergative pattern; and the pronominal clitics, which operate according to the split-S system. Although they are autonomous, both systems can operate simultaneously, as can be observed from (19)-(24), resulting, as a consequence, with the coreference between free forms and clitics. A question may be raised here as to how this could be handled in a minimalist framework, in which Case and agreement are to be checked under the same structural relations.[15]

[15] According to Chomsky (1992), Case assignment is a manifestation of the Spec-head relation. He proposes two different AGR positions if two NPs in VP require structural Case: AGR_S or AGR_O. If VP contains only one NP, one of the two AGR elements will be active. If the choice is AGR_S, the single NP will have the properties of the subject of a transitive clause; if the choice is AGR_O, it will have the properties of the object of a transitive clause. These two possibilities result in nominative and ergative languages, respectively.

Everett (1996) assumes a model with no typological distinction between AGR nodes. Instead, he proposes a model in which distinctions in syntactic behavior are based only on configurational positions, so that he takes AGR as a node without any typing of different kinds of AGRs. Morphological subcategorization will indicate how many AGR positions the verb has. And a parsing principle, which accounts for the configurational distance agreement between the verb and nominals in the clause (CDAP), will tell which nominals are most in need of being marked on the verb, that is, those which are configurationally more distant from the verb at PF. It is worth noting that he also makes use of notions such as anaphoric index and relativized minimality (to distinguish between AGR positions locally), in conjunction with the notion of theta-coindexation (to account for ergative languages) in the formalization of CDAP. Grammaticality contrasts follow from this principle so that AGR can surface either as clitics or agreement affixes, depending on morphological subcategorization. Affixes are m-subcategorized, while clitics are not. This difference plays a role in Case assignment. According to Everett, the Spec-head relation is not the only option available, since non-m-subcategorized AGR nodes represent a variation on the possible conditions for AGR manifestations and functions.

A look at the facts of Marubo is needed from one or another point of view, since it may have consequences in respect to these matters. Nevertheless, it seems that neither of the proposals manage to explain the semantic/pragmatic basis underlying the coexistence of the ergative and the split-S system in the language. A more related approach under the Minimalist program is pursued by Uriagereka (1995). According to him, "special" clitic placement follows from the syntax of specificity and referentiality. He proposes that languages may have an active or inactive site peripheral to the sentence, which he calls F (cf. Uriagereka 1988, 1992, *apud* Uriagereka 1995). In his view F syntactically encodes a speaker's or an embedded subject's point of view. It is seen as a point of interface at LF between the competence levels of syntax and the performance levels of pragmatics. He then argues that languages with an active F overtly place clitics in this site, while languages with an inactive F employ other strategies. Parametric differences in clitic placement follow from the activity and from the morphological weight of F.

3.2.2. Split conditioned by tense, aspect and modality

As we saw above, Marubo is an ergative language regarding nominal case-marking. Free-form (pro)nouns in A function are marked by the ergative case; and those that are in S and O function are marked by the absolutive. In certain constructions, however, nominal case-marking operates according to the nominative-accusative system. This kind of split is motivated by the tense, aspect and modality system (TAM system, cf. Givón 1984).

Events (dynamic situations seen as single complete wholes), processes (dynamic situations seen in their internal temporal structure), or states can be interpreted as established or completed situations; as habitual or continuous, transitory or permanent situations; as predictable or potential situations (cf. Comrie, 1976). Different ways of referring to different situations may be coded by means of lexical items, by means of lexically composite expressions, or by means of grammatical categories. The notions of tense, aspect and modality are generally indicated on the verb by verb morphology, but they can also be coded by lexical items, such as temporal adverbs; by lexical expressions, as some aspectual markers; or by grammatical words adjacent to the verb, as in the case of auxiliaries and modals (cf. Comrie 1985).

Splits may arise from the interaction between the case-marking system and the TAM system, so that certain constructions obey the ergative pattern while others follow the accusative pattern, depending on the kind of situation being expressed by the construction in question. As pointed out by De Lancey (1981, 1982, 1985) the perfective and imperfective, as well as volition and control, are categories that crucially determine splits in ergative languages. So, different syntactic strategies are employed to differentiate situations that are initiated and controlled by a participant from situations that involve or affect a participant, in such a way that it is now identified with S and A (as an agent initiator and controller of the situation), now with S and O (as a non-controller or non-intentional participant, or as a patient affected by the situation). These situations may refer to events, processes or states that took place in the past; take place in the present; and may take place in the future. The same situations may be seen in their internal or external temporal structure, so that they can be interpreted as a complete whole (perfective aspect), on the one hand, or as recurrent customary situations, or situations that occur continuously along time (imperfective aspect), on the other. These situations may, finally, involve limited observations about the real world (realis modality) or generalizations about possible worlds (irrealis modality).

As pointed out by Dixon (1994: 99), many languages may obviously show nominative-accusative marking in all aspects and tenses, while others show absolutive-ergative unimpeded by aspect or tense. But if a language shows a split conditioned by tense or aspect, the ergative marking is always found either in past tense or in perfective aspect. According to Dixon, "ergative marking is most likely to be found in clauses that describe some definite result, in past tense or perfective aspect. An ergative system is less likely to be employed when the clause refers to something that has not yet happened (in future tense), or is not complete (imperfective aspect) or did not happen (negative polarity), or where there is emphasis on the agent's role (imperative or hortative moods)" (p. 101).

In Marubo the ergative marking is employed in the present, past and future to refer to dynamic situations (events and processes). This type of marking is independent of person and number. First, second and third persons, singular or plural, are treated the same way, according to the ergative marking. Thus, actions that happened in the past, actions that did not happen yet, but will happen in the future, and actions that happen in the present moment are constructed on an ergative basis. In the same way, processes that are developing in the present moment, or even in the past, are also constructed according to the ergative marking.

Events and processes are coded in the same way in Marubo: that is, there are no aspectual distinctions concerning complete actions and actions in progress. Present tense has as reference point the moment of utterance (**now**), the deictic temporal center in relation to which situations are located, but it is actually used to refer to situations that occupy a longer period of time than the present moment. In particular, it is used to speak of situations that hold at the day of **today**. It is coded morphologically by the suffix **-ai** (also pronounced as [a]) to indicate *momentaneous present* or *immediate past* (the past of today), as can be seen in:

(41) ɯ̆ˈẽ̄ ˈmī̆ă ɯ̃ˈw̃īẽĩ
ɨˈan ˈmia-ø ɨn-ˈwin-**ai**
I-ERG you-ABS 1A-see-PRES/IM.PAST
'I see you.'

(42) măˈtũ̄ ˈnẽ̄mĭ ˈpīă
maˈtu-n ˈnami-ø ˈpi-**ai**
you(PL)-ERG meat-ABS eat-PRES/IM.PAST
'you eat meat.'

(43) tʃẽˈnũ̄ mẽˈsɯ̃̄ ˈpākɯ̆ăɩ
tʃaˈnu-n manˈsɨn-ø ˈpakɨ-**ai**
PN-ERG bowl-ABS throw-PRES/IM.PAST
'ˈtʃanu has thrown the bowl.'

(44) mĭ'ẽ̄ 'nūkɯ̆ mĩʃŭ'tũẽĩ
mi'an 'nukɨ-ø min-ʃu'tun-**ai**
you-SG-ERG we-ABS 2A-SG-push-PRES/IM.PAST
'You have pushed us.'

Present is in a sense a neutral tense in Marubo. It is employed to refer to actions that happen or happened *today/now*. But it does not exclude the *progressive* and the *habitual* sense, as can be observed from the following examples:

(45) mă'nĩʃĩnĩ ẽ'ātsă 'nĩsă
ma'niʃi-nin an-'atsa-ø 'nisa-**ai**
PN-ERG 3A-SG-cassava-ABS rasp-PRES/IM.PAST
'ma'niʃi is rasping cassava.'

(46) nŭ'kɯ̃ 'nẽmĭ nũ'pĩă ʃă'vā'tũtũtă'kĩmă
nu'kɨ-n 'nami-ø nun-'pi-**ai** ʃa'va'tuntunta'kima
we-ERG meat-ABS 1A-PL-eat-PRES/IM.PAST every day
'we eat meat every day.'

(47) mă'yẽ̄ 'pẽ̄nĭ 'kɯ̄kɯ̆ăɩ
ma'ya-n 'pani-ø 'kɨkɨ-**ai**
PN-ERG net-ABS weave-PRES/IM.PAST
''maya is weaving a net.'

In Marubo there are many tense markers that code *past* tense, which is subdivided into various degrees of distance in the time scale. By the use of these markers it is possible to allude to situations that happened *yesterday*, *some days ago*, *months (or moons) ago*, *years ago*, *decades ago*, *centuries ago*, and *a long, long time ago*. Below are examples of the use of two of these suffixes:

(48) ɯ̆'ẽ̄ mĩ'pẽ̄nĭ ɯ̃'māʃtɯ̆văɩ năʃă'vāmă
ɨ'a-n min-'pani-ø ɨn-'maʃtɨ-**vai** na-ʃa'va-ma
I-ERG 2-POSS-net-ABS 1A-finish-REC.PAST DEM-day-NEG
'I finished your net yesterday.'

(49) ɯ̆'ẽ̄ 'ʃōpă 'ātă'rāyănă'mẽ̄ʃɷ̆ ɯ̃'wĩ̄ʃ'nā
ɨ'a-n 'ʃopa-ø 'ata'raya-na'man-ʃu ɨn-'win-ʃ'**na**
I-ERG PN-ABS city noun-LOC-PROV 1A-know-REM.PAST
'I came upon 'ʃopa in Atalaia (moons/years ago)'

Only one tense marker is used to locate a situation in a time subsequent to the present moment, indicating *immediate* or *remote future*:

(50) ˈɐ̃̄tũ kăˈpɯ̄ ˈyɐ̃̄mămă ˈkātsĕɩ
ˈan-tun kaˈpɨ-ø ˈyamama-ˈ**katsai**
he-ERG alligator-ABS kill-FUT
'He will kill the alligator.'

As can be seen from the data above, all of these tense markers do occur in ergative constructions. The split takes place in constructions that describe situations with a continuous, stable, permanent temporal structure. The *continuous*, non-progressive imperfective aspect is coded in Marubo by the aspectual marker **-mis**, used for situations that refer to general truths that hold at all times and are not restricted temporarily. Along with the aspectual marker, the *present* tense marker **-ka** is used to refer to situations that occupy a much longer period of time than the present moment, but which include the present moment within them. This marker is also used in adjectival forms that denote *inherent qualities* or *permanent states*, that is, states that are maintained in the present, but which have started before the present moment and may extend beyond the present (see 30). This can be observed in the following examples:

(51) ˈyūɾă ˈnɐ̃̄mĭ pĭˈmī̆skă
ˈyura ˈnami pi-ˈ**mis-ka**
people meat eat-CONT-PRES
'People eat meat.'

(52) ˈa kăˈpɯ̄ ˈyɐ̃̄mămăˈmī̆skă
ˈa kaˈpɨ ˈyamama-ˈ**mis-ka**
he alligator kill-CONT-PRES
'He always kills alligator.'

The data above show that such kinds of constructions deviate from the ergative pattern, operating according to the accusative system.[16]

[16] If we consider morphological marking we may say that such a system is *neutral* in that the same morphological marking (here a null one) is used for all three syntactic positions S, A and O. As assumed by Comrie (1978: 340), "the neutral nominal case-marking is compatible with either a nominative-accusative or an ergative-absolutive system, in that it does not make any distinction cutting across either of these two distinctions." As shown below, when we consider word order as well as some syntactic aspects (cf. Section 4), we see that the constructions in question operate on a nominative-accusative basis.

Another tense marker in Marubo, the suffix **-ya**, occurs in adjectival forms denoting a *quality resulting from a change of state*, that is, a quality or state resulting from a process that leads to a well-defined terminal point, beyond which the process can not continue, although the resulting final state is maintained in the present moment and may extend beyond the present moment (see 31 and 32). This marker also occurs with stative intransitive or transitive verbs. Compare (31) and (32) with the sentence below, which shows a stative transitive verb and is constructed according to the accusative pattern.

(53) ˈyūɾă ˈvō măˈpū̄ ˈāyă
ˈyura ˈvu maˈpu-n ˈa-**ya**
people hair head-LOC AUX (T)(=have; exist)-PRES
'People have hair on the head.'

The same suffix can be used to stativize active constructions, be they transitive or intransitive, in which case it may be analyzed also as a nominalizing suffix (cf. 4.1). In this usage those constructions describe continuous, generic or customary actions that are related to recurrent past actions, and which are reinterpreted as quality rather than activity. The following data exemplify this usage:

(54) ˈʃāɩɾĭˈs̄̄ĩɾω̆ ‿ ˈnūyăyă
ˈʃai-riˈsin-ru ˈnuya-**ya**
bird-PL-TOP fly-PRES/NOM
'Birds fly (As for the birds, they fly.).'

(55) ˈnūkɯ̆ ˈāskătă ˈẽ̄tsămăʃtă ˈpīăyă
ˈnukɨ ˈaskata ˈantsa-ma-ʃta ˈpia-**ya**
we always a lot-NEG-DIM eat-PRES/NOM
'We always eat little.'

(56) ˈpūyă tăˈwẽ̄ ˈyāpă ˈākăyă
ˈpuya taˈwa-n ˈyapa ˈa-ka-**ya**
PN arrow-INSTR fish AUX(T)(=fish)-PRES-PRES/NOM
'ˈpuya fishes with arrow.'

These data show that S (in 54) is treated equally as A (in 55 and 56). Again, as is the case of (51) and (52), we have a split in the ergative system, conditioned by tense and aspect. Now operates the nominative-accusative system, where the grammatical relations are established just by means of word order: SV order for intransitive sentences and AOV order for transitive ones.[17]

In respect to modality, a component of the TAM system, it is also responsible for splits in the ergative system. As noted by Givón (1984: 272), "modality encompasses among other things our notions of **reality**, in the sense of 'having factual existence at *some* real time' ('true'), 'having existence at *no* real time' ('false'), or 'having *potential* existence in some *yet-to-be* time' ('possible')." The affirmative sentence codes a true proposition, while the negative sentence codes a false proposition; and different types of constructions are used to refer to possible realities. In Marubo, the nominative-accusative pattern is conditioned by *negation* and by the *impossibility* of realization of a situation. According to Dorigo and Costa (1996 a), the negation marker **-ma** is a sentence final operator, which is attached to the main verb or to an auxiliary as a suffix. In the same way, impossibility is marked by the modal operator **-tinpa**. When these two particles attach themselves to verbs,

---

[17] In sentences in which the ergative-absolutive system operates word order is not fixed, admitting variations, generally for discursive reasons, among the pragmatically neutral order SOV and the OSV, SVO and OVS orders. This flexibility is constrained in cases of split ergativity, in which the SOV order is rigid, since it is the only means of case-marking core arguments.

The flexibility observed in word order when the ergative system operates, in the face of its rigidity in the cases of splits, has been in fact linked to morphology in Costa (1992): in sentences in which the ergative-absolutive axis operates, morphology acts, setting the order free. On the other side, in the nominative-accusative axis, the order operates as a case-marking device, from which results its rigidity.

With the attempt to relate several problems resulting from the functionalist approach, adopted in Costa (1992), in recent works (cf. Costa 1993, 1996 b) we turn the analysis to a formal perspective, having as support recent developments of generative theory. We depart from the assumption that the variation in constituent order can be derived from a highly constrained set of simple parameters, which interact with universal principles of human language.

In order to reach an explanation for the morphological coincidence between ergative subject and genitive, locative, instrumental, means and genitive-possessive case-marking (cf. Footnote 8); to establish a relationship between constituent order variation and case-marking devices; and, finally, to put in question the syntactic position of what we have been calling "object" and "ergative subject", we postulate that "the syntactic representation bears the existence of an external argument, which, necessarily marked by morphology, is opposed to internal arguments, which, being assigned structural case, dispense with morphological marking."

Pursuing this hypothesis, we intend to deeply analyze the tense, aspect and modality system, as long as conclusions about the existence of a functional complex in the language may have consequences for Case assignment.

some aspect and tense marks that appear in the correspondent affirmatives may vanish in certain cases (realis modality: past and present tense, cf. 57 and 58), while others are retained (irrealis modality: continuous aspect and future tense, cf. 60 and 62). In the case of tense morphemes, if they are expressed they are attached to the auxiliary (cf. 62).

In transitive sentences negation and impossibility imply the non-realization of an activity. In these cases A does not control the situation, being thus identified with S. Identified as S, A is marked like S, therefore according to the accusative marking. Observe in the examples below the identification between S and A, where A is distinguished from O only through AOV (except for (61), with right dislocation of P).

Intransitive sentences

(57) ˈā ˈrẽ̄mă ˈūʃămă
ˈa ˈrama ˈuʃa-**ma**
he today sleep-NEG
'He did not sleep today.'

(58) ˈʃāɩ ˈnūyătīpă
ˈʃai ˈnuya-**tinpa**
bird fly-IMPOS
'The bird can not fly.'

Transitive sentences

(59) măˈyẽ̄pă ˈnẽ̄mĭ pĭˈāmă
maˈyanpa ˈnami piˈa-**ma**
PN meat eat-NEG
'maˈyanpa does not eat meat.'

(60) ˈa kăˈpɯ̄ ˈyẽ̄măm ăˈmīsmă
ˈa kaˈpɨ ˈyamama-ˈmis-**ma**
he alligator kill-CONT-NEG
'He never kills alligator.'

(61) ˈɯ̄ă ˈmāʃtɯ̆mă ⌢ ˈpẽ̄nĭ
ˈɨa ˈmaʃtɨ-**ma** ˈpani
I finish-NEG net
'I have not finished the net.'

(62) ˈɯ̃ă mẽˈsɯ̄̃ păˈkɯ̄mă ˈīkătsĕɩ
ˈɨa manˈsɨn paˈkɨ-**ma** ˈi-katsai
I bowl throw-NEG AUX(I)-FUT
'I will not throw the bowl'

(63) ˈmātŏ ˈɾẽ̄tʃă tʃĭˈvẽ̄tĩpă
ˈmatu ˈrantʃa tʃiˈvan-**tinpa**
you-PL boat reach-IMPOS
'You can not reach the boat.'

(64) ˈɯ̃ă mẽˈsɯ̄̃ ˈvīɩnă tĩpă
ˈɨa manˈsɨn ˈvi-ina-**tinpa**
I bowl lead-DIR-IMPOS
'I can not lift the bowl up'

From the facts considered up to this point, we conclude that the ergative marking is employed in transitive constructions that describe dynamic situations, with or without internal temporal structure, which may effectively happen in the past, in the present and in the future. The splits conditioned by the TAM system occur in sentences that refer to static, continuous, incomplete situations (present, imperfective), or to situations that in reality did not happen or are impossible to happen (negation, impossibility). The accusative pattern operates in such constructions.

4. Syntactic aspects

In the previous sections we saw that the nominal case-marking in simple clauses obeys the ergative pattern, with manifestations of the accusative pattern conditioned by the TAM system. In this section we consider complex sentences in order to see if there are constraints in combinations of different kinds of clauses and whether such possible constraints are based on semantic factors or are grammatically conditioned splits.

When two clauses are linked by coordination or subordination, two types of syntactic constraints may occur: those regarding the combination of certain types of clauses and those associated with the omission of coreferential constituents in clause combination. If these constraints treat S and O equally, distinctly from A, the language operates with the **S/O** pivot. If they treat S and A equally and O differently, the language operates with the **S/A** pivot. In the first case the language is said to be "syntactically ergative"; in the second, it is said to be "syntactically accusative" (cf. Dixon 1994:143).

The term "pivot" (introduced by Dixon 1979) is a syntactic category that describes the syntactic equivalence between S and A or between S and O. According to Dixon (1994:156), "pivot" and "subject" are distinct syntactic categories. S, A and O are universal syntactic relations, which are applicable at both underlying and derived syntactic levels. "Subject" is a universal category that links together A and S at the underlying structure level. "Pivot" is a language-particular category that operates at the level of derived structure with two possibilities of identification: S/A or S/O.

A pivot constraint may be invoked when two clauses are combined to form a complex sentence. If the language operates according to the S/A pivot, a common NP can only be omitted from one of the clauses if it is in S or A function in each of the clauses. If the language operates in terms of the S/O pivot, a common NP can only be omitted from one of the clauses if it is in S or O function in each of them.

In order to satisfy such conditions, the language has syntactic mechanisms, like the passive and the antipassive. Passive puts an underlying O NP into derived S function and demotes A, which can still be omitted. Antipassive puts an underlying A NP into derived S function and demotes O, which can also be omitted. One of the functions of passive or antipassive is to "feed" a syntactic pivot. Passive feeds an S/A pivot, satisfying the requirement that coreferential NPs be in S or A function. Antipassive feeds an S/O pivot, which requires that coreferential NPs be in S or O function, so that two clauses can be linked and/or the omission of one of them may occur (p. 143-144).

Dixon (1994) adds that not all languages operate in terms of pivot, showing then no syntactic constraints in clause combination. The possibility of omission of a coreferential NP is achieved by other mechanisms, like word order, verbal agreement, switch-reference marking (coded through verbal inflection, to indicate that coreferential NPs are or are not in a derived S/A function, cf. p. 153), or simply according to the semantic nature of constituents. Thus, splits between different types of clauses, which are apparently a grammatical conditioning phenomenon, are, in certain cases, associated to semantic factors and are conditioned by the distinction between types of NPs and by the TAM system (p. 101).

In what follows we intend to test certain predictions proposed by Dixon (1994) about universal tendencies that certain types of subordinate clauses show of being constructed according to one or another case-marking pattern, which may lead to a split in relation to the main clause. We want to check the point at which such expectations are attested in Marubo. Searching for syntactic motivations for the split in the language, we also intend to verify whether or not it operates in terms of pivots, or if other mechanisms apply in clause combination. To do that we will examine three types of constructions: *relative clauses*, *purposive clauses* and *coordinate clauses*.

4.1. Relative clauses

As Dixon (1994:102-103) observes, relative clauses detail an action that takes place at the same time or before the event referred to by the main clause, and the event described by the relative clause is related to an NP in the main clause. He expects that if there is a split in morphological marking between main clause and relative clause, the relative clause will show an ergative pattern, while the main clause will be of the nominative type. According to him, the reason for the ergative bias in relative clauses is that they resemble past tense (or perfective) main clauses in describing something that has happened or is happening. Further, relative clauses with a "restrictive" meaning specify more fully the referent of the noun they qualify and can only be used with nouns or plural pronouns, not with first or second person singular, which are already fully specified. Relative clauses thus tend to be associated with NPs that are located at the right-hand end of the Nominal Hierarchy, which is in turn associated with ergative marking..

In Marubo, the relativization of an NP in S, A or O function is accomplished through nominalization of intransitive or transitive constructions, by the addition of the nominalizing suffix **-ya**. As seen in 3.2.2, this suffix is also an aspectual marker, which occurs with stative verbs and in adjectival forms denoting quality or change of state. The "relative clause" in Marubo is actually a nominal construction consisting of a transitive or intransitive construction plus a nominalizing morpheme.[18] Such a construction functions as an adjective, a nominal head modifier. The head is not morphologically marked, no matter what type of structure is modifying it. Here we have a split from the ergative to the accusative pattern: A and O are distinguished, to the extent of the complex NP internal structure, through AOV order. AOV order is neutral in discourse-pragmatic terms in Marubo. Intransitive constructions show the neutral SV order.[19] These can be observed in (65) and (66) below:

---

[18] Nominalizing constructions corresponding to "relative clauses" can also be observed in Tikuna (an isolated language), as pointed out by Soares (1990:103-106), as well as in a number of other Amazonian languages.

[19] The existence of a neutral order in discourse-pragmatic terms has syntactic implications, insofar as precedence (linearity) may be relevant for certain control relationships (see 4.2, example 73).

(65) ˈvākɯ̆ mɯ̆sˈtɯ̄̃kă ˈwāɪmătʃĩ ˈmɯ̄ĭ ˈkīyă
[ˈvakɨ $_S$ mɨsˈtɨn-ka ˈwai-matʃi ˈmɨ-i-ˈki-**ya**] $_A$
child strong-PRES-PERM garden-on work-AUX(I)-PRES-NOM

ˈnāwĭ kɯ̆ˈyūkĭ ˈtʃāʃăɪvɯ̆̃
ˈnawi $_O$ kɨˈyuki ˈtʃaʃa-ai-vu
grass all clean-PRES/IM.PAST-PL
'The strong boys who work on the garden have cleaned all the grass.'

(66) ˈɾūnɯ̆̃ ˈɯ̄ă ˈnāʃăvăyă ˈʔɛ̄̃nĭkă
[ˈrunu $_A$ ˈɨa $_O$ ˈnaʃa-vai-**ya**] $_S$ ˈani-ka
snake I bite-REC.PAST-NOM big-PRES-PERM
'The snake which bit me was big.'

Considering the clause where the NP as a whole functions as S, A or O, we find both the ergative and accusative patterns. If the complex NP is O, it is distinguished from A through the ergative marking in A, in which case the order is set free, since it may vary as seen in:

(67) ˈwɛ̄̃tū ˈvɯ̄̃nɯ̆ɾĭsĩ nŭˈkūvăˈɾɛ̄̃yă tăˈnāɪ
ˈwan-tun $_A$ [ˈvɨni-rasin $_S$ nŭˈku-vaˈran-**ya**]-ø $_O$ taˈna-ai
He-ERG man-PL arrive-MOV-NOM-ABS count-PRES/IM.PAST
'He has counted the men who arrived.'

(68) ˈʃɨ̄̃nĭwɯ̆tsă ĭʃˈnā ˈʃūpă mɯ̆ˈtʃāvăyă
[ˈʃini-wɨtsa $_A$ iʃˈna ˈʃunpa $_O$ mɨˈtʃa-va-ya]ø $_O$
old-someone bad papaya tree pull-REC.PAST-NOM-ABS

tʃɛ̄̃ˈnū̃ ˈyɛ̄̃mămăɪ
tʃaˈnu-n $_A$ ˈyamama-ai
PN-ERG kill-PRES/IM.PAST
'ˈtʃanu has killed the bad old man who pulled the papaya tree out.'

Nevertheless, if the complex NP is A, two possibilities are found: (a) it is distinguished from O by AOV order, revealing thus an accusative pattern, as can be observed in (65) above; (b) it is marked by the ergative case, as in (69) below:

(69) ˈvɯ̃̄nɯ̆ ˈyūɾă ˈātĭ ˈākăyătũ
[ˈvɨnɨ $_A$ ˈyura $_O$ ˈati $_O$ ˈa-ka-**ya**]-**tun** $_A$
man person harm AUX(T)-PRES-NOM-ERG

ˈvākɯ̆ ˈwāɩmăɩ
ˈvakɨ-ø $_O$ ˈwai-ma-ai
child-ABS cry-CAUS-PRES/IM.PAST
'The man who does harm to people has made the children cry.'

Thus, both case-marking and word order allow for the identification of A and O in the transitive clause. We see then that there is a fluctuation in the choice of one or another system to the extent of the whole sentence. It seems that this fluctuation is due to the kind of function of the NP in the relative construction. If it is in S function in the relative clause, as in (65), the main clause shows an accusative pattern; if it is in A function in the relative clause, as in (69), the main clause is constructed in an ergative pattern.

The fact that Marubo shows a split in the ergative pattern, both in the range of the relative clause and in the range of the main clause, is against Dixon's expectation that relative clauses have an ergative bias, inasmuch as they resemble past tense (or perfective) main clauses in describing something that has happened or is happening. In the case of Marubo, the **-ya** marker is used, on the contrary, to denote qualities or present states resulting from past actions, thus conditioning the accusative pattern. Nevertheless, Dixon's expectation that the split is associated with semantic factors and is not syntactically motivated is confirmed.

4.2. Purposive clauses

According to Dixon (1994:102), purposive clauses normally refer to some attempt at a controlled action and generally have an A or S agent NP that is coreferential with some NP in the main clause. For this type of subordinate construction he expects S and A to be treated in the same way within the complement clause. But if there is a split in case-marking between main clause and purposive clause, the expectation would be that the subordinate shows the accusative pattern while the main clause requires an ergative pattern. This is because purposive clauses resemble main clauses in future tense (or imperfective aspect), in the sense that they express some potential event as a propensity of the agent, and thus demand accusative marking.

In Marubo the purposive clause is constructed by the replacement of tense inflection on the verb with the particle **-nun**, which indicates *volition* and may also carry the notion of *futurity*. In general, this particle expresses the future and volitional intention of S or A (in some data, the tense marker -

katsai is used instead of **-nun**). It may also be the case that the postposition **ʃu**, indicating *provenience*, may occur along with **-nun** (cf. Costa 1992: 155-162). This postposition indicates that the subordinate clause is the causing source of the action carried in the main clause. The postposition **inan**, which express purpose, is located at the end of the subordinate clause.

The main clause is constructed according to the ergative pattern. In Marubo there is no syntactic mechanism constraining the control of a coreferential NP deletion in a subordinate clause. The deleted NP can have any of the functions—A, S and O—in the subordinate clause, whether it is in A, S or O function in the main clause. As a consequence, this allows for the identification between S and A, as well as the identification between S and O.

The identification between S and A can be observed in the examples below (where **e** stands for the deleted NP). In (70) the main clause is transitive and the subordinate is intransitive, with A_1=S_2. In (71), S_1=A_2:

(70) măˈyẽ̄ ˈɾāω ˈāvăɩ ˈvōnũ ĭnẽ
$_{A1}$ maiˈya-n$_i$ $_{O1}$ ˈrau-ø ˈa-vai $_{S2}$ **e**$_i$ ˈvu-nun-inan
PN-ERG medicine-ABS AUX(= drink)-REC.PAST heal-VOL-PURP
ʻˈmaya$_i$ drunk medicine **e**$_i$ to heal.'

(71) ˈtʃẽ̄nω̆ ɯ̆ˈɾɯ̄văɩ ˈɾẽ̄tʃă
$_{S1}$ ˈtʃanu-ø$_i$ ɨˈrɨ-vai $_{A2}$ **e**$_i$ $_{O2}$ ˈrantʃa-ø
PN-ABS run-REC.PAST boat-ABS

tsɯ̆ˈkɯ̄kăˈĩ̄ẽ tʃĭ̃ˈvẽ̄nũ ĭnẽ
tsɨˈkɨ-kaˈin-ai tʃiˈvan-nun-inan
depart-MOV-PRES/IM.PAST reach-VOL-PURP
ʻˈtʃanu$_i$ ran **e**$_i$ to reach the boat that was leaving.'

The identification between S and O may be seen in (72), where O_1=S_2:

(72) ɯ̆ˈẽ̄ ˈnũ̄tĭ ɯ̃ˈātʃ ĭvăˈĩ̄ĕɩ
$_{A1}$ ɨ-ˈan$_j$ $_{O1}$ ˈnunti-ø$_i$ ɨn$_j$-ˈatʃi-vaˈin-ai $_{S2}$ **e**$_i$
I-ERG canoe-ABS 1A-hold-MOV-PRES/IM.PAST

păˈkɯ̄kʷẽ ˈmīsĭ ĭnẽ
paˈkɨ-kawan-ˈmisi-inan
fall-MOV-PREV-PURP
'I held the canoe$_i$ to prevent **e**$_i$ from falling.'

This example is ambiguous regarding the reference of the deleted NP. S_2

might refer either to O_1 or to A_1, since an agent can hold something to prevent either the thing or himself from falling. In this case, then, the reference of the omitted NP can only be recovered by the situational context. The ambiguity that may arise in cases like this may, however, be eliminated in Marubo if the order of the clauses is reversed so that the reference of the deleted NP is made explicit in the subordinate clause. This is the case of (73) below, where the subordinate precedes the main clause. Here S_2 occupies the sentence initial position, the topic position, and the omitted NP is the one in the main clause (surely O_1, not A_1).

(73) ˈvākŭĭ ˈwāĭˈmīsĭĭnẽ ˈvũ̄ ˈīkɯ̃nĭĕɩ
$_{S2}$ˈvakɨ-ø$_i$ ˈwai-ˈmisi-inan $_{A1}$ˈvu-n $_{O1}$**e**$_i$ ˈikuni-ai
child-ABS cry-PREV-PURP PN-ERG take-PRES/IM.PAST
'To prevent the child$_i$ from crying, ˈvu took **e**$_i$.'

In this case, constituent order, as long as clauses are concerned, along with ergative case-marking in A_1, allow for the identification of O_1 as coreferential to S_2. It seems from this example that linearity also plays a role in control relationships, since it contributes to disambiguation of the omitted NP reference. It is worth observing that the modal -**misi**, cliticized to the verb, indicates that A_1's purpose is to attempt to avoid the event expressed by the verb; that is, the purpose of A_1 is to block the possibility that O_1 *fall* (cf. (72) or *cry* (cf. (73)).

The examples below show other possible combinations between main and purposive clauses which support evidence for the absence of syntactic constraints in this kind of construction in Marubo. In (74), S_1=S_2; in (75), O_1=A_2. Finally, (76) includes two deleted NPs in the subordinate clause–A_2 and O_2, coreferential to A_1 and O_1, respectively.

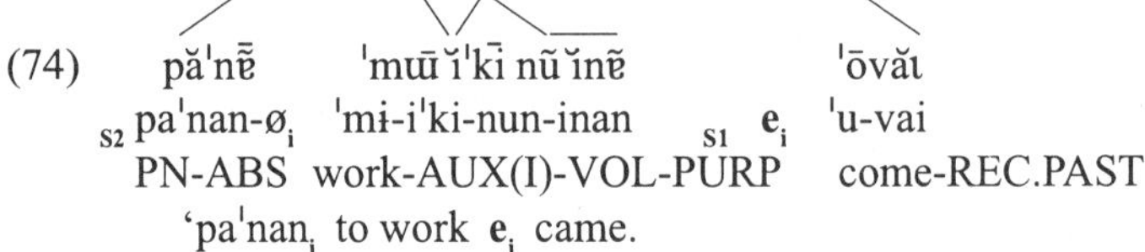

(74) păˈnẽ ˈmɯ̃ĭˈkĩ nũĭnẽ ˈōvăɩ
$_{S2}$paˈnan-ø$_i$ ˈmɨ-iˈki-nun-inan $_{S1}$ **e**$_i$ ˈu-vai
PN-ABS work-AUX(I)-VOL-PURP come-REC.PAST
'paˈnan$_i$ to work **e**$_i$ came.

(75) vɯ̆ˈtẽ̄wẽ ẽˈvā kɯ̆ ˈyūnɯ̆ăɩ
$_{A1}$vɨˈtanwa-n $_{O1}$an-ˈvakɨ-ø$_i$ ˈyunu-ai $_{A2}$**e**$_i$ $_{O2}$
PN-ERG 3-POSS-daughter-ABS order-PRES/IM.PAST

ˈwākăpăʃă vĭˈtẽ̄nũĭnẽ
ˈwakapaʃa-ø vi-ˈtan-nun-inan
water-ABS lead-MOV-VOL-PURP
'vɨˈtanwa told her daugther$_i$ **e**$_i$ to get water.'

(76) mă'nĩʃĭnĩ 'yāpă 'ʃōιĕι 'pĩnω̆ʃω̆ĭnẽ
$_{A1}$ ma'niʃi-nin$_i$ $_{O1}$ 'ya pa-ø$_j$ 'ʃui-ai $_{A2}$ **e**$_i$ $_{O2}$ **e**$_j$ 'pi-nu-ʃu-inan
PN-ERG fish-ABS roast-PRES/IM.PAST eat-VOL-PROV-PURP
'ma' niʃi$_i$ is roasting fish$_j$ **e**$_i$ **e**$_j$ to eat.'

From the data examined to this point, we see that it is possible to combine main and purposive clauses without needing an operation to derive S from A or O. In summary, the language does not operate with pivots in purposive subordinate clauses. This fact is in accordance with Dixon's expectation that S and A are treated in the same way within the complement clause.

4.3. Coordinate clauses

We saw that Marubo shows no syntactic constraints in combining main and purposive clauses. We saw that clause order and case-marking contribute to the identification of omitted NPs.

We now turn to coordination. Considering this type of construction, one can not think about tendencies to one or another system, since coordination involves just the combination of two ore more independent clauses. It is in this type of construction that we can verify if Marubo is ergative at the inter-clause syntactic level. If there are constraints regarding NP deletion, and if these constraints require a pivot, then we can state that the language is syntactically ergative or syntactically accusative; in the first case, it should manifest an S/O pivot; in the second, an S/A pivot. Showing the existence of a pivot, it will certainly have mechanisms to derive S from O or from A

Coordination in Marubo is accomplished without any overt conjunction[20] simply by juxtaposing two sentences, with omission of the appropriate NP from one of the clauses, generally the second one (but see 84 below, with the omission of the first A NP). It can also be accomplished with the intercalation of a clause between S or A and the predicate. Tense markers or other particles may be used to indicate the sequentiality of the events being carried by each clause.

We exemplify some simple sentences before examining their syntactic behavior in coordination. (77) and (78) are examples of intransitive and transitive simple sentences.

(77) 'yūɾă 'nω̄nω̆ 'ūă
$_S$ 'yura-ø 'nɨnu 'u-ai
man-ABS here come-PRES/IM.PAST
'The man has come here.'

[20] Marubo is similar to Dyrbal in that there is no overt particle to indicate coordination, which "is recognized by the whole complex making up one intonation group and by the omission of the second occurrence of the NP in pivot function" (cf. Dixon 1994:162).

(78) yŭ'ɾẽ̄ ă'ī̄ vŏ̄ 'ɾī̄ʃkĭĕɩ
$_A$ yu'ra-n $_O$ a'invu-ø 'riʃki-ai
man-ERG woman-ABS hit-PRES/IM.PAST
'The man has hit the woman.'

There is neither passive nor antipassive in Marubo. The function of focusing O, instead of A, is accomplished through OAV or AVO order (notice also the use of a pause separating the focused element from the rest of the sentence), with the maintenance of ergative marking in A, as can be seen in:

(79) ă'ī̄ vŏ̄ ‸ yŭ'ɾẽ̄ 'ɾī̄ʃkĭ kŭ̄'kū̄văɩ
$_O$ a'invu-ø $_A$ yu'ra-n 'riʃki-kɨ'kɨ-vai
woman-ABS man-ERG hit-ITER-REC.PAST
'The woman, the man has hit.'/ 'The woman was hit by the man.'

(80) yŭ'ɾẽ̄ 'ɾī̄ʃkĭ kŭ̄'kū̄văɩ ‸ ă'ī̄ vŏ̄
$_A$ yu'ra-n 'riʃki-kɨ'kɨ-vai $_O$ a'invu-ø
man-ERG hit-ITER-REC.PAST woman-ABS
'The man has hit, the woman.' / 'The woman was hit by the man.'

Although the language lacks syntactic mechanisms like passive or antipassive, it allows for the identification between S an A, as well as the identification between S and O in coordination processes. The sentence below shows a combination in which S=A and is constructed simply by juxtaposition. The transitive clause precedes the intransitive, so that A_1 is case marked by the ergative morpheme, and S_2, the common NP in the second clause is omitted. The sequentiality of the events is marked in each clause by tense markers (**-vai** in the first clause denotes recent past (from yesterday backwards); **-ai** in the second clause indicates present or immediate past (the past of today).

(81) yŭ'ɾẽ̄ ă'ī̄ vŏ̄ 'ɾī̄ʃkĭ kŭ̄'kū̄văɩ ‸
$_{A1}$ yu'ra-n$_i$ $_{O1}$ a'invu-ø 'riʃki-kɨ'kɨ-vai $_{S2}$ **e**$_i$
man-ERG woman-ABS hit-ITER-REC.PAST

'nū̄nŏ̄ 'ūă
'nɨnu 'u-ai
here come-PRES/IM.PAST
'The man$_i$ hit the woman and **e**$_i$ came here.'

The same occurrence of events may be constructed with the intercalation of the antecedent clause between S and the predicate, as can be seen in (82) below, where A_2 is deleted, instead of S_1.

(82) ˈyũɾă ăˈĩ vɷ̆ ˈɾĩʃkĭvăˈɾẽĩ
ˈyura **e** aˈinvu-ø ˈriʃki-vaˈran-ai
S1 man-ABS A2 i O1 woman-ABS hit-MOV-PRES/IM.PAST

ˈnɯ̃nɷ̆ ˈũă
ˈnɨnu ˈu-ai
here come-PRES/IM.PAST
'The man$_i$ **e**$_i$ hit the woman and came here.'

The sequentiality between the clauses is marked in this case by the tense suffix **-ai**, in both verbs, and by a particle that indicates movement and direction, which is attached to the transitive verb (see also 67 above). These types of markers have as a reference point the place where the speaker is at the moment of speech. They can also be used metaphorically as temporal markers. Marking the verb, the particle **vaˈran** in (82) indicates that the event carried by *hit* is anterior to the event of *coming*. Now if the event of *coming* is prior to the action of *hitting*, the same kind of construction can be made with the intercalation of the intransitive clause between A and the predicate, as in:

(83) yŭˈɾẽ ˈnɯ̃nɷ̆ŏˈʃũ ăˈĩ vɷ̆ ˈɾĩʃkĭ kɯ̆ˈkɯ̃ăĩ
A1 yuˈra-n$_i$ S2 **e**$_i$ ˈnɨnu u-ˈʃu O1 aˈinvu-ø ˈriʃki-kɨˈkɨ-ai
man-ERG here come-PROV woman-ABS hit-ITER-PRES/IM.PAST
'The man$_i$ **e**$_i$ came here and hit the woman.'

Here S_2 is the omitted common NP. The sequentiality is indicated by the postposition **Su**, which denotes provenience. When used in coordination, this postposition indicates that the event carried by the verb marked by it precedes the one expressed in the other clause.

From these two types of constructions—juxtaposition and intercalation—we see that the combination between S and A may be accomplished in any order: A_1S_2 or S_1A_2. The choice depends on the kind of construction and on the perspective of the speaker in what event he judges as more relevant.

The identification between S and O can be observed in the following sequence of clauses:

(84) ˈũpɷ̆ ˈtʃũʃtăkă ˈwĩnẽ
O1 ˈunpu-ø$_i$ ˈtʃuʃtaka A1 **e**$_j$ ˈwin-nan A2 **e**$_j$ O2 **e**$_i$
clothes-ABS dirty see-FOC

ɯ̃ ˈtʃākăɪ ˈr͂ēmărɷ̃ ˈtʃūʃtămă
ɨn_j-ˈtʃaka-ai ˈramaru $_{S3}$ $\mathbf{e}_i$ ˈtʃuʃta-ma
1A-wash-PRES/IM.PAST now dirty-NEG
'$\mathbf{e}_j$ seeing the dirty clothes$_i$, $\mathbf{e}_j$ have washed; now, $\mathbf{e}_i$ are clean.'

In (84), $O_1=O_2=S_3$, and O_2 and S_3 are deleted. Further, A_1 and A_2, coreferential to each other, are also deleted, but they can be recovered by the pronominal clitic on the verb. It is worth attempting the fact that both A and S_a can be identified by pronominal clitics. Nevertheless, even when clitics do not occur, the omission of NPs in different functions is possible. In (85), for example, $O_1=A_2=S_3$. All of the three NPs are deleted, but their reference as third person is inferred (the absence of a third person pronoun in Marubo is very common).

(85) ŭɪˈẽ ɯ̃ˈkūnăɪ ăsˈkāmɯ̃kĩ
$_{A1}$ ɨˈa-n_j $_{O1}$ $\mathbf{e}_i$ ɨn_j-ˈkɨna-ai asˈkamɨnkin $_{A2}$ $\mathbf{e}_i$
I-ERG 1A-call-PRES/IM.PAST but

nĩˈk͂ēmăʃɷ̃ ŭˈāmă
ninˈkan-ma-ʃu $_{S3}$ $\mathbf{e}_i$ uˈa-ma
listen-NEG-PROV come-NEG
'I have called $\mathbf{e}_i$ but $\mathbf{e}_i$ did not listen; so $\mathbf{e}_i$ did not come.'

As we saw, any NP, as far as S, A and O are concerned, may be omitted in Marubo, no matter the function of the coreferencial NP in the other clause. Then, any kind of identification between coreferencial NPs is allowed: S=A, S=O and even A=O. We conclude that Marubo is a language with no syntactic constraints in relation to coordination and subordination. The absence of pivots explain the absence of mechanisms such as passive or antipassive. A common NP may be omitted not according to a syntactic rule, but by means of other strategies like constituent order and case-marking itself. Pronominal clitics also contribute to the identification of a deleted NP. Therefore, Marubo can not be classified either as "syntactically ergative" or as "syntactically accusative." The manifestations of ergativity are confined exclusively to the morphological level in this language.

5. Final remarks

Considering the facts of Marubo examined here, we summarize below our conclusions.

According to Costa (1992), we have shown that Marubo is an ergative language, which uses combinations among morphology, nasalization and stress as case-marking devices. The ergative marking is also manifested in free-form pronominals, in all persons, singular and plural. Although closely related to agentivity, there are also motivations for the ergative marking in Marubo.

Ergative marking is employed in transitive constructions that describe dynamic situations, with or without internal temporal structure, and which may effectively happen in the past, in the present and in the future. However, there are splits conditioned by tense, aspect and modality. In this case, the accusative pattern, which is coded simply by word order, takes place. This system is manifested in clauses referring to static, continuous, incomplete situations (present, imperfective); or to situations that actually did not happen (negation) or cannot happen (impossibility). As for pronominal clitics, which are attached to the verb or to the direct object for phonological reasons, the language operates according to the split-S system. Although Dixon (1994) considers this system as a split between the ergative and the accusative systems, we concluded that, in Marubo, the split-S system functions independently from the ergative system. As autonomous systems, both can operate simultaneously and, as a result, the coreference between free-form (pro)nominals and pronominal clitics may occur in simple or complex sentences.

Sentences containing a nominal head modified by a nominalized construction ("relative clause") show an accusative pattern—grammatical relations are established only by constituent order. Considering the clause in which the "relativized NP" functions as S, A, or O, we found a fluctuation between the ergative and the accusative system—both nominal case-marking and constituent order make possible the identification between A and O in the transitive sentence.

In Marubo there are no syntactic constraints in respect to the combination between main and purposive subordinate clauses. The order of the clauses as well as case-marking contribute to the identification of deleted NPs.

Although the language does not have syntactic mechanisms such as passive and antipassive, any kind of identification between coreferential NPs is possible in coordinate clauses: S=A, S=O and even A=O. So any NP, whether in S, A or O function, may be deleted, no matter the function of the coreferential NP in the other clause. The absence of pivots justify the absence of mechanisms such as passive and antipassive. The identification between coreferential NPs is achieved by means of constituent order and nominal case-marking. Pronominal clitics, operating according to the split-S system, along with ergative marking, do also contribute to the identification of an omitted NP. And, in certain cases, ambiguities are resolved by the situational context. We can finally conclude that Marubo can not be classified either as "syntactically ergative" or as "syntactically accusative," but as a "morphologically ergative" language.

Deeper syntactic analyses of ergative languages alongside the development of typological studies may lead to an exact syntactic definition of languages that share this type of case-marking. Here we leave our contribution.

References

Boutle, Philip Ernest. 1964. Formulário Padrão (163 items). Cruzeiro do Sul: Acre.

Cavuscens, Silvio and Lino J. O. Neves. 1986. Povos Indígenas do Vale do Javari (elaboration). Campanha Javari. Manaus:CEDI.

Chomsky, Noam. 1992. A Minimalist Program for Linguistic Theory. MIT Occasional papers in Linguistics 1.

Clements, G. N. 1989. A Unified Set of Features for Consonant and Vowels. Ms., Cornell University.

_______. 1993. Lieu d'articulation des consonnes et des voyelles: une théorie unifiée. Architeture des Représentations Phonologiques, eds.B. Laks and A. Rialland. Paris: CNRS Editions.

_______ and E. Hume. 1995. The Internal Organization of Speech Sounds. The Handbook of Phonological Theory, ed. J. Goldsmith. Cambridge and Oxford: Blackwell.

Comrie, Bernard. 1976. Aspect: an Introduction to the Study of Verbal Aspect and Related Problems. Cambridge: Cambridge University Press.

_______.1978. Ergativity. Syntactic Typology: Studies in the Phenomenology of Language, ed. W.P. Lehman, 329-394. Austin: University of Texas Press.

________.1985. Tense. Cambridge: Cambridge University Press.

Costa, Raquel Guimarães R. 1992. Padrões Rítmicos e Marcação de Caso em Marubo (Pano). MA thesis. Rio de Janeiro: UFRJ.

_______. 1993. A Conexão Sintaxe-Fonologia em Marubo (Pano). Research project for Doctoral degree. Rio de Janeiro: UFRJ.

_______. 1996a. The Encoding of Deictic Elements in Marubo (Pano). Paper presented at the 1995-96 Annual Meeting of the Society for the Study of the Indigenous Languages of Americas (SSILA), in conjunction with the Annual Meeting of the Linguistic Society of America. San Diego, California.

_______. 1966b. Aspectos da Gramática Marubo (Pano). To appear in Anais do XI Encontro Nacional da ANPOLL (Associação Nacional dos Programas de Pós-Graduação em Letras e Lingüística). João Pessoa, Paraíba.

Deibler, E. W. 1966. Semantic Relationships of Gahuku Verbs. SIL and Norman: University of Oklahoma.

De Lancey, Scott. 1981. An Interpretation of Split Ergativity and Related Patterns. Language 57, no. 3: 626-657.

_______. 1982. Aspect, Transitivity and Viewpoint. Tense-Aspect: Between Semantics and Pragmatics, 167-183. Edited by P. Hopper. Amsterdam/Philadelphia: John Benjamins Publishing Company.

_______. 1985. On Active Typology and the Nature of Agentivity. Trends in Linguistics - Studies and Monographs 2: 47-60. Mouton Publishers.

Dixon, R.M.W. 1979. Ergativity. Language 55:59-138.

_______. 1994. Ergativity. Cambridge Studies in Linguistics 69. Cambridge: Cambridge University Press.

Dorigo, Carmen Teresa and Raquel Guimarães R. Costa 1996 a. Aspectos de la Negación en Matsés y Marubo (Pano). Paper presented at Jornadas de Antropologia de La Cuenca Del Plata - II Jornadas de Etnolingüística. Facultad de Humanidades y Artes de la Universidad Nacional de Rosario.

_______. 1996 b. Constituintes Métricos nas Línguas Matsés e Marubo (Pano). To appear in Anais do VI Congresso da ASSEL-Rio, UFRJ.

Everett, Daniel L. 1987. Pirahã Clitic Doubling. Natural Language and Linguistic Theory 5:245-76.

_______.1989. Clitic Doubling, Reflexives, and Word Order Alternations in Yagua. Language 65:339-72.

_______.1996. Why There Are No Clitics: An Alternative Perspective on Pronominal Allomorphy. Publications in Linguistics 123. SIL and The University of Texas at Arlington.

Franchetto, Bruna, Márcia D.Vieira and Yonne de F. Leite. A Ergatividade nas Línguas Indígenas Brasileiras: um Estudo Morfossintático. Ms., Rio de Janeiro: UFRJ.

Givon, Talmy. 1984. Syntax: A Functional-typological Introduction I. Amsterdam, Philadelphia: John Benjamins Publishing Company.

Hale, K. L. 1973. Person Marking in Walbiri. A Festschrift for Morris Halle, ed. S. R. Anderson and P. Kiparsky, 308-44. New York: Holt, Rinehart and Winston.

Halle, M. and J. R. Vergnaud. 1987. An Essay on Stress. Cambridge:MIT Press.

Hayes, Bruce. 1991. Metrical Stress Theory: Principles and Case Studies. Ms., UCLA.

Jaeggly, Oswaldo. 1982. Topics in Romance Syntax. Dordrecht: Foris.

Jelinek, Eloise. 1984. Empty Categories, Case and Configurationality. Natural Language and Linguistic Theory 2:39-76.

Kaisse, E. M. 1982. Sentential Clitics and Wackernagel's Law. Proceedings of the First West Coast Conference on Formal Linguistics, eds. D. P. Flickinger, M. Macken and N. Wiegand, 1-14. Stanford:Stanford University.

_______. 1985. Connected Speech. The Interaction of Syntax and Phonology. New York:Academic Press.

Leite, Yonne de F. 1990. Para uma Tipologia Ativa do Tapirapé: Os Clíticos Referenciais de Pessoa. Cadernos de Estudos Lingüísticos 18:37-56. Campinas:UNICAMP.

Liberman, M and A. Prince. 1977. On Stress and Linguistic Rhythm. Linguistic Inquiry 8: 249-336.

Mithun, M. 1984. The Evolution of Noun Incorporation. Language 60: 847-95.

Nespor, Marina and Irene Vogel. 1989. On Clashes and Lapses. Phonology 6:69-116.

Sadler, Louisa. 1988. Welsh Syntax: A Government-binding Approach. London: Croom Helm.

Schutze, Carson T. 1993. Towards a Minimalist Account of Quirky Case and Licensing in Icelandic. MIT Working Papers in Linguistics 19: Papers on Case and Agreement II, 321-375.

Soares, Marília F. 1990. Marcação de caso e Atribuição de Caso em Tikuna. Cadernos de Estudos Lingüísticos 18:79-114. Campinas:UNICAMP.

_______. 1992. O Suprassegmental em Tikuna e a Teoria Fonológica. Volume I: Aspectos da Sintaxe Tikuna. Volume II: Ritmo. PhD dissertation. Programa de Pós-Graduação em Lingüística. IEL. Campinas:UNICAMP.

_______.1996. Aspectos Lineares e Não-lineares de Processos Fonológicos em Línguas Indígenas Brasileiras. Letras de Hoje 31(2): 77-96. Porto Alegre: PUC.

_______. (to appear). A Contribuição do Tikuna às Regras do Ritmo e à Relação Sintaxe-Fonologia. Estudos de Prosódia no Brasil. ed. Ester M. Scarpa. Campinas:Editora da UNICAMP.

_______, Raquel Guimarães. R. Costa , and Carmen T. D. de Carvalho. 1993. Para uma Classificação Rítmica das Línguas Pano. Special publication of Signo and Seña, Instituto de Lingüística, Faculdad de Filosofia y Letras, Buenos Aires.

Suner, Margarita. 1990. The Role of Agreement in Clitic Doubling Constructions. Natural Language and Linguistic Theory 6: 391-434.

Uriagereka, Juan. 1995. Aspects of the Syntax of Clitic Placement in Western Romance. Linguistic Inquiry 26.1:79-123.

Appendix: Aspects of Marubo phonology

Detailed information on Marubo phonology was approached in Costa (1992). It consists of a linear analysis, which has recently been reviewed under a non-linear point of view. Some of the results accomplished in respect to rhythm and stress can be seen in Soares, Costa and Carvalho (1993), as well as in Dorigo and Costa (1996 b). In what follows we summarize the main phonological facts which may be helpful in understanding the paper.

Consonantal and vocalic systems

In a phonological analysis that only seeks contrast, the following consonantal and vocalic phonemes can be established for Marubo, as represented in Tables 1 and 2.

	labial	*alveolar*	*alveopalatal*	*palatal*	*velar*
stop	p	t			k
nasal	m	n			
fricative	v	s	ʃ		
affricate		tʃ	tʃ		
tap		r			
approximant	w			y	

Table 1: Consonantal system

	front	*central*	*back*
high	i	ɨ	u
low		a	

Table 2: Vocalic system

If the contrasts observed in the language are conceived in terms of the features system proposed by Clements (1989, 1993) and Clements and Hume (1995), Marubo consonants and vowels can be seen, regarding local constriction, as in Tables 3 and 4 below.

	/p/	/t/	/k/	/m/	/n/	/v/	/s/	/ʃ/	/tʃ/	/r/	/w/	/y/
labial	+			+		+					+	
coronal		+			+		+	+	+	+		+
anterior[21]		+			+		+	-	-	+		-
dorsal			+									

Table 3: Consonantal system

	/i/	/ɨ/	/u/	/a/
labial			+	
coronal	+			
dorsal		+	+	+
[opened 1]	-	-	-	+

Table 4: Vocalic system

Segmental alterations

Consonants

Consonants undergo the following processes:

(a) Prenasalization with voicing

In the beginning of a non-initial syllable word, and preceded by a nasalized vowel, /k/ may be realized as [ᵑg], as in:

(01) [mũ̆sˈtũ̄ĩkă] [mũ̆sˈtũ̄ĩᵑgă] 'strong'

(b) Partial denasalization

In the beginning of a non-initial syllable word, /m/ and /n/, followed by an oral vowel, may be realized as [ᵐb] and [ⁿd], respectively, as in:

(02) [ˈvimi] [ˈvĩ̄ᵐ**b**i] 'fruit, proper noun'

[ˈtʃẽ̄nŏ] [ˈtʃẽ̄ᵑ**d**o] 'proper noun'

---

[21] In Clements & Hume (1995), [anterior] is a subarticulatory feature of [coronal].

(c) Voicing

When preceded by a nasalized vowel, from which it is separated by a morpheme boundary, /ʃ/ may be realized as [ʒ]:

(03) [pă'nĩ̄+ʃɯ̆̃] [pă'nĩ̄+ʒɯ̆̃] 'in a hammock'

In intervocalic position, in a stressed syllable (after a syllabic segment fall), /s/ tends to be realized as [z], as in:

(04) ['ɐ̃̄tsămă'ʃtāsɨ̆ 'ā yă] ['ɐ̃̄tsămăʃtă'**z**āyă] '...there is little'

/s/ is realized as [z] before a nasal consonant (according to our data, when there is a morpheme boundary between them), as in:

(05) ['vɐ̃̄năs+mă] ['vɐ̃̄nă**z**+mă] '... do not talk'

(d) Labialization

According to our data, this process involves two specific syllable beginnings—/k/ and /w/—and occurs in fast speech when, after a vocalic segment fall, /k/ and /w/ are in contact, from which results the realization [kʷ], as in:

(06) [pă'kɯ̃̄kɐ'wɐ̃̄ĩ̄] [pă'kɯ̄'**kʷ**ɐ̃̄ĩ̄] 'It fell down.'

Vowels

The following general phonological processes can be found in respect to vowels:

(a)Raising/lowering

In general, high vowels are lowered and tense vowels are laxed. The central vowel is backed and/or lowered in unstressed syllables. And the low vowel is raised and/or fronted before /i/ (also realized as [i]), both constituting a phonetic diphthong,[22] and resulting from partial assimilation to the preceding syllable vowel, from which it is separated by a morpheme boundary. A trend to vocalic harmony is found throughout the system.

(b) Nasalization

There are no nasal vowels from the phonological point of view. Vocalic nasalization is due to: (a) vowel contact with an immediately following nasal

[22] The vowels /i/ and /u/ may constitute a falling diphthong with a preceding vowel. /i/ can form a diphthong with /a/ and /u/; /u/ can form a diphthong with /a/ and /ö/.

consonant; (b) nasality spreading from left to right; and (c) nasality spreading from right to left.

Soares (1996) reanalyzes data from Costa (1992) from a non-linear point of view. In this type of analysis the process needs, for its expression as obligatory or facultative, the intervention of an entity that is present in the non-linear representation—the syllable. There is much work in respect to nasality in Marubo. The systematization found in Soares (1996) can be summarized as follows:

Nasalization by vowel contact with the nasal consonant at the onset of the following syllable, as in:

(07) /ˈina/ [ˈĩ nă] 'tail' /ˈvɨnɨ/ [ˈvɯ̃nɨ̆] 'man'

/ˈrunu/ [ˈɾũnŏ] 'snake' /yaˈmɨ/ [yẽˈmɯ] 'night'

/ˈranɨ/ [ˈɾẽnɯ̆] 'adornment' /ˈʃumu/ [ˈʃũmŏ] 'pot'

/ˈrɨmu/ [ˈɾɯ̃mŏ] 'tobacco' /ˈimi/ [ˈĩmĭ] 'blood'

Nasalization by vowel contact with the following consonant in the coda, as in:

(08) /iˈan/ [ĭˈẽ] 'lake' /tɨˈan/ [tɯ̆ˈẽ] 'small river'

/aˈin/ [ăˈĩ] 'woman, wife, female'

Vocalic nasality obtained by contact with a nasal consonant that constitutes the ergativity morpheme:

(09) [ˈyũʃĩ] 'proper noun' [yŭˈʃĩ] PN-ERG /yuˈʃi-n/

[ˈyũɾă] 'man' [yŭˈɾẽ] man-ERG /yuˈra-n/

[ˈvõ] 'proper noun' [ˈvũ] PN-ERG /ˈvu-n/

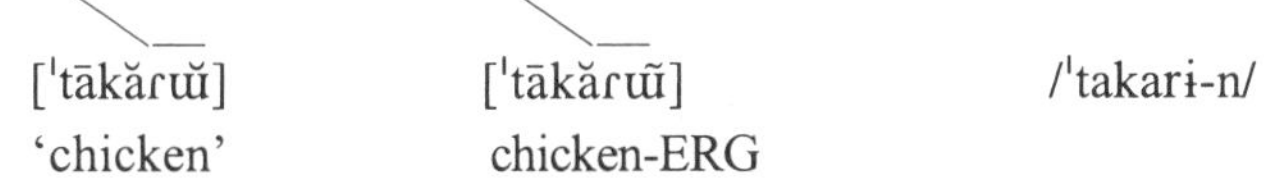

['tākărɯ̆] ['tākărɯ̃] /'takarɨ-n/
'chicken' chicken-ERG

Stress and nasalization

In respect to a possible relationship between stress and nasalization in Marubo, Soares (1996:93) states, based on Costa (1992), and from data like the ones below, that "in forms that are marked with the ergative case, and which correspond to non-ergative forms with second syllable prominence, the apparent systematic nasalization observed in the first vowel followed by a nasal consonant at the subsequent syllable onset position could be related to a possible intervention of stress."

(10) [pă'nɐ̃̄] ['pɐ̃̄nănɯ̆] / ['pɐ̃̄nɐ̃̄nɯ̆] /pa'nan-n/
'proper noun' PN-ERG

[kă'mɐ̃̄] ['kɐ̃̄mɐ̃̄nɯ̆] /ka'man-n/
'jaguar' jaguar-ERG

[ɾɨ̆'kĩ̄] ['ɾɨ̃kĩ̄nɯ̆] /rɨ'kin-n/
'nose' nose-ERG

This interpretation, advanced in Costa (1992), is supported, according to Soares (1996), by the distinction found in the language between systematic nasalization and facultative nasalization: the first is conditioned by a nasal consonant at the coda and the second, by a nasal consonant at the onset. As the kind of nasalization in question—the one observed in the examples above—is systematic, despite being conditioned by a nasal consonant at the onset, it is possible that it is favored by stress intervention. Such a possibility, still following Soares (1966:92), "should be checked with data specifically related to nasalization, and which, above all, take into account a possible variation, regarding vocalic nasalization, in ergative forms of the language."

Rhythm and Stress

An analysis of metrical constituents, based on a version of metrical stress theory, namely "bracketed metrical grid", proposed by Hayes (1991), was accomplished in Dorigo and Costa (1996b). Here we present some of the results obtained.

The main stress prosodic correlate in Marubo is *high pitch*, combined with greater duration and intensity. The language ignores syllable internal structure. It does not take into account the distinction between light and heavy syllables, being then "quantity insensitive." Five rhythmic patterns were found in simple words, at the level of phonetic realization, as can be seen in:

(11) a. σ b. σ σ c. σ σ d. σ σ σ e. σ σ σ

'nĩ 'vɯ̃nĩ kă'pɯ̃ 'ɾāvŭʃɯ̆ mɯ̃'tsĩsĭ

'grass' 'man' 'alligator' 'knee' 'nail'

As we consider binary and ternary patterns, both with initial prominence (cf. 11 b and d) as the most general in the language (since they are by large more frequent), we can establish *syllabic trochees* as basic metrical feet for the language, which are constructed from left to right, with End Rule left (main stress assignment), as can be seen in:

(12) a. (x)
(x .)
σ σ
'wākă
'water'

b. (x)
(x .)
σ σ σ
'tākăɾɯ̆
'chicken'

Feet are constructed non-adjacently, according to the weak local parsing, the marked value of the Foot Parsing Locality Parameter (cf. Hayes1991: 258), that is, they can be separated from each other by a single mora (in effect, a single light syllable). Weak local parsing then accounts for the ternary pattern, as seen in (12 b), (the last syllable of which is a light syllable skipped over by the parsing algorithm).[23]

Morphological complex words show three or more syllables, the first two constituting the root, added by one ore more suffixes, as can be observed in (13). Depending on the number of the added suffixes, the complex word may show: (a) subordination of the added syllables to the root stressed syllable (cf. 13 a, b and c); (b) not only stress on the root, but also on the penultimate syllable of the derived word (cf. (13 d). There are then two types of stress in Marubo: lexical stress and the stress derived from rhythmic regulation.

[23] The other patterns showed in (11) can be derived by other mechanisms such as the allowance of degenerate feet (feet consisting of a single syllable), as in 11 a and c, and initial extrametricality (the first syllable is invisible for purposes of creating metrical structure), as in 11 c and e. As Hayes (1991) suggests that initial extrametricality may be vanished from extrametricality theory, we are at present in pursuit of other mechanisms to explain the coexistence of trochees and iambs in Marubo, inasmuch as both patterns are crucially involved in case-marking, as shown in 3.1.1.

(13) a. 'ẽ̄tsă-**kă** 'a lot'
a lot-PRES-PERM

b. 'ẽ̄tsă-**mă** 'a little'
a lot-NEG

c. 'ẽ̄tsă-**mă-ʃtă** 'a little'
a lot-NEG-DIM

d. 'ẽ̄tsă-**mă-"ʃtā-sɨ̆** 'a little'
a lot-NEG-DIM-MAN

The presence or absence of stress on the suffixes can be explained if we assume that the rules of stress assignment operate in two levels in Marubo: at the level of the root, with *lexical stress* assignment (represented as '); and at the level of rhythmic regulation, with *phrasal stress* assignment (represented as "). This last one may manifest over a prosodic group, comprised either by a longer word or by more than one lexical item. Stress assignment rules that apply to the forms examined so far are posited as follows:

Level 1: lexical stress rules

Form a syllabic trochee from left to right, obeying the weak local parsing parameter.
Degenerate feet are allowed in strong position.
Word layer: End Rule left.

Level 2: Phrasal stress rules (rhythmic regulation)

Form a syllabic trochee at the end of the word from left to right, obeying the weak local parsing parameter.
Degenerate feet are forbidden.
Phrasal layer: End Rule right.

With foot parsing at level 1 and the assignment of End Rule left we get the results in (12) and the following outputs for the words in (14) a, b and c, respectively ( ] demarcating the right edge of the root):

```
(14) a. (x      )    b. (x      )   c. (x          )      word layer
        (x  .)          (x  .)         (x  .)             foot layer
        σ  σ  σ         σ  σ  σ        σ  σ  σ  σ
        'ẽ̄tsă]kă        'ẽ̄tsă]mă       'ẽ̄tsă]măʃtă
            ↓               ↓              ↓  └→ computed
        non-computed    non-computed   non-computed
```

In these words syllables that are not analyzed at level 1 will be parsed only with the operation of level 2 rules. A syllabic trochee can be constructed at the end of the word, from right to left and non-adjacently to the initial foot. With the weak local parsing, the syllable adjacent to the root (**-ka** in 14 a and -

ma in 14 b and c), glossed as "non-computed", is ignored in foot construction. The following syllable (**ta.**[24] in 14 c) is available for foot construction, but can not be parsed because at level 2 degenerate feet are prohibited. Nevertheless, if one more suffix is added to the root, as is the case of **-sɨ** in (15), a syllabic trochee can be parsed at the end of the word, as can be observed in (15 a). (15 b) shows the final derivation, with phrasal End Rule right assignment.[25]

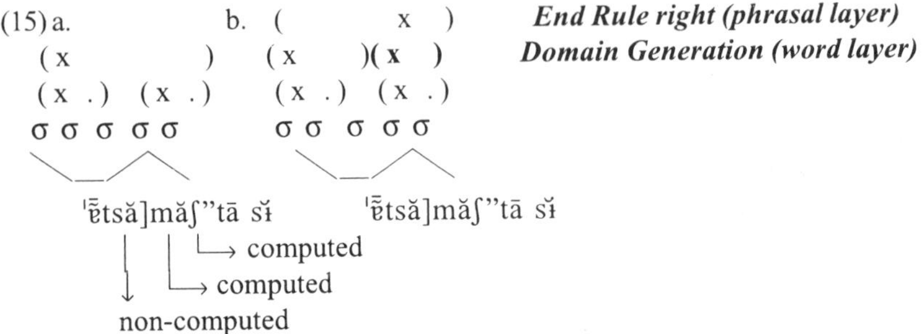

Stress assignment at level 2 goes beyond word level and may apply to phrases and sentences, provided that the number of syllables in a prosodic group is sufficient for the assignment of metrical structure rules (cf. Dorigo and Costa 1966b).

Concerning rhythm and stress typology, Marubo can be classified as a bounded, quantity insensitive system. It is a syllabic-trochaic language, with foot parsing from left to right at the word level and from right to left at the phrasal level. As for main stress assignment, it shows initial stress at the word level and final prominence at the phrasal level.

Abbreviations

A	transitive subject function
ABS	absolutive
ASSOC	associative
AUX	auxiliary
CAUS	causative
CONT	continuative

[24] Here the suffix **-ʃta** is resyllabifyed when it is added into the word, as can be better seen in (15).

[25] As the first syllable shows a higher grid assigned by lexical End Rule, it is necessary to apply Domain Generation over the final trochee (as seen in bold in 15 b) so that End Rule right can be assigned without violating the Continuous Column Constraint (cf. Hayes 1991:319).

DEM	demonstrative
DIM	diminutive
DIR	direction
EMPH	emphatic
ERG	ergative
FOC	focus
FUT	future
I	intransitive
IM. PAST	immediate past
IMPOS	impossibility
INSTR	instrumental
ITER	iterative
LOC	locative
MAN	manner
MOV	movement
NEG	negation
NOM	nominalization
O	transitive object function
PERM	permanent
PL	plural
PN	proper noun
POSS	possessive
PRES	present
PREV	prevention
PROV	provenience
PURP	purpose
REC. PAST	recent past
REFL	reflexive
REM. PAST	remote past
RES	resultative
SG	singular
S	intransitive subject function
S_a	intransitive subject marked like transitive subject
S_o	intransitive subject marked like transitive object
T	transitive
VOL	volitive

The acoustic correlates of stress in Pirahã

Keren Madora Everett

University of Pittsburgh

1. Introduction

The main focus of this paper is to investigate the acoustic correlates of stress in Pirahã for the purpose of understanding how fundamental frequency (F0) is used for stress and tone. Pirahã is a language which has tone and predictable stress (Everett 1986). It is a tone language in the sense that F0 is lexically contrastive for each vowel of a word (Pike 1948). The important phonetic facts being considered are that the acoustic correlates of stress in Pirahã are greater amplitude and duration, not F0, and F0's main function is to indicate lexical contrasts.

This study is organized into four major sections. In the first section a brief historical background on the phonetics of stress is given, along with an introduction to the Pirahã people and language. The second section outlines the procedures used in this study. The third section presents the results of an acoustic study of amplitude, duration, fundamental frequency and formant frequencies of stressed and unstressed syllables, and compares these results to the phonetics of stress for the language types of stress-accent, pitch-accent and tone languages. The final section discusses the implications of these findings for understanding the phonetics of stress, and suggests possible further research on both the phonetics of stress and the phonetics of tone in relation to F0.

1.2. Brief historical background on the phonetics of stress and fundamental frequency

Most studies of stress by early descriptive linguists were done only of English. These studies claimed that the stress/non-stress distinction within a language was acoustically a difference in amplitude (Bloomfield 1933 and Trager and Smith 1951). It was assumed that the stress distinction was directly related to the degree of force used by the speaker, while intonation was directly related to pitch (Kingdon 1958a; 1958b). This position was challenged in the late '50s, and early '60s by perceptual experiments showing that the most effective means by which speakers produce and perceive stress in English are respectively, changing pitch, duration and intensity (Fry 1955;

[JAL, vol. 1, no.2, March1998, pp. 104-162]

1958; 1965, Mol and Uhlenbeck 1956). Based on these studies Bolinger (1958) was the first to demote intensity to the role of a quality-enhancing helper and to equate stress directly with fundamental frequency. Bolinger's claims about the phonetics of stress for English were generalized to other languages. Hadding-Koch's (1961) exhaustive experimental study of Southern Swedish showed that F0 played a dominant role in stress judgments. Rigault (1962) showed the same for French. As the phonetic constraint of equating stress with F0 was extended to other languages, it became clear that stress systems and tone systems in any given language could not be distinguished on the basis of phonetic correlates alone, as both are dependent on F0 (Hyman 1978). Thus the ambiguity arises, one that this study seeks to investigate: How are stress and tone systems phonetically distinguishable, given that both are equally dependent on F0?

Some linguists have handled the ambiguity created from stress and tone systems that are equally dependent on F0 by raising the question as to whether stress and tone can co-occur in a 'real' tone language (Pulleyblank 1983). In autosegmental phonology the ambiguity is handled with a definition of accent which reserves a formal place within the word for some basic tone shape (Goldsmiths 1976; 1982). In this definition, the phonetics of stress are equated with the acoustic correlate of F0 (tone shape). While this disambiguates how stress systems and tone systems interact with respect to F0, a clear concern that develops from such a definition, one that will be discussed in this study, is that there is no phonetic distinction established between stress-accent, pitch-accent language and tone languages, other than the degree to which F0 is functionally used in the language. So English, a stress-accent language, can be described as a 'tone' language because it uses tone shapes whose phonetic content is exactly that of contrastive tones in a tone language, namely, fundamental frequency (Goldsmith 1976; 1982).

All treatments of the phonetics of stress that claim F0 is the primary acoustic correlate of stress do not help to clarify the phonetics of stress in Pirahã because stress is independent of F0. Such treatments also make Pirahã's classification as a tone language a phonetically insignificant and uninformative classification, in that the basic phonetic content of stress in stress-accent languages and pitch-accent languages is the same as that of contrastive tones in a tone language. As will be seen in this study, there is very little similarity between Pirahã's use of F0 for stress and tone and the use of F0 for stress and tone in stress-accent and pitch-accent languages.

1.3. The Pirahã language

1.3.1. The Pirahã language and people

There are approximately 250 Pirahã. It is difficult to do a census because the Pirahã are semi-nomadic, located on the Maici River, a tributary of the Madeira River. Pirahã is the only language spoken in the region of the Maici

River. The location of the Pirahã is seen in Figure 1.

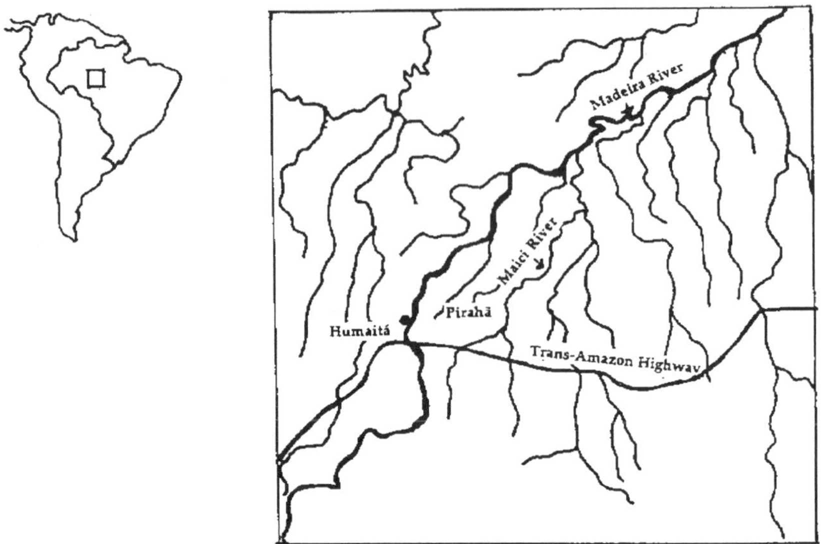

Figure 1:Location of the Pirahã along the Maici River

The Pirahã language has traditionally been referred to as the Mura-Pirahã (Everett 1986). This designation obscures the distinction between the Mura language family and the Mura and Pirahã languages. The Mura family has no known external affiliates and it includes Pirahã and three dead languages: Matanawi, Bohura and Yahahi (Everett 1986).

1.3.2. Pirahã Phonology

This section provides a brief description of the phonemes, stress and tones in Pirahã.

Segments

Pirahã has one of the smallest segment inventories ever documented. There are eight consonants and three vowels. The consonants are presented in Table 1.

	bilabial	*alveolar*	*velar*	*glottal*
plosives	/p/	/t/	/k/	/ʔ/
	/b/		/g/	
fricatives		/s/		/h/

Table 1: Pirahã consonants

The vowels are: /i/, /a/ and /o/. The six diphthongs and monophthongs arising from the combination of the three vowels in complex nuclei are illustrated in Table 2.

a.	ao vs. oa	
	bàó!sàì	'clothes'
	?i!tòábi	'to open'
b.	ia vs. ai	
	!káìpì	'to make'
	?ì!gíàbì	'similar'
c.	oi vs. io	
	kòí	'really'
	?ì!gìó	'with'
d.	i vs. ii	
	?ì!tì	'face'
	?ìì!tíì	'battery'
e.	a vs. aa	
	!kàbà	'not'
	!kààbáòbí	'to bite'
f.	o vs. oo	
	!?òbí	'to throw'
	tòò!tòò	'duck'

'!' precedes stressed syllable
´=high tone
`=low tone

Table 2: Monophthongs and diphthongs

Syllable structure

The basic syllable types in Pirahã are (C)VV and CV. There are no complex onsets and no coda positions in the language. A single vowel cannot function as a syllable.

Stress

In Pirahã stress is assigned on the basis of syllable weight and syllable position. Syllable weight is determined by a combination of both the onset and nucleus of a syllable. Syllables with voiceless onsets are heavier than syllables with voiced onsets. In addition, syllables with long vowels and diphthongs are heavier than syllables with short vowels. These two weight criteria interact to produce the following ranking of syllables for stress assignment, where C is voiceless and G is voiced:

CVV>GVV>VV>CV>GV

Using this hierarchy the stress will fall on the heaviest syllable nearest to the end of the word in the domain of the last three syllables.

The following pairs of words illustrate changes of stress placement. In a) and c), stress is assigned to the first syllable because CV is heavier than GV. In b) and d), syllable weight does not help to determine stress placement because both syllables are equal in weight. For these two words it is the syllable closest to the end of the word that will receive stress.

a. !kàbà 'not'	!CVGV
b. gà!bà 'a small fruit'	GV!GV
c. !pìgì 'swift'	!CVGV
d. bò!gì 'chest'	GV!GV

For a more thorough phonological analysis of stress in Pirahã, see K. Everett (1978), D. Everett (1979; 1988), and D. Everett and K. Everett (1984a).

Lexical tone

Pirahã is a tone language with two contrastive tones, a high and a low (Everett 1979). All vowels must be specified for tone. Pirahã does not have toneless syllables. There are four possible tone patterns for monosyllabic words as seen in a. through d. and four tone patterns for non complex, disyllabic CVCV words as seen in e) through h) of Table 3.

a. tí	high	'me'(object)
b. tì	low	'I'(transitive subject)
c. hòí	low-high	'many'
d. hóì	high-low	'few'
e. !tígí	high	'small parrot'
f. !tìgì	low	'hard'
g. kà!pí	low high	'coffee'
h. tí!hì	high low	'tobacco'

Table 3: Basic tone patterns of monosyllabic and disyllabic words with simple nuclei

Tone is independent of stress in Pirahã. In particular, the assignment of tone is not influenced by the stress of the word. In the following table, the four basic tone patterns for disyllabic CVGV versus CVCV words are illustrated. a) through d) and e) through h) demonstrate the same four tone patterns, but a) through d) have penultimate stress while e) through h) have final stress.

a. !tígí	high	'small parrot'	!CVGV
b. !pìgì	low	'swift'	!CVGV
c. !sàbí	low-high	'mean'	!CVGV
d. !?ábì	high-low	'to stay'	!CVGV
e. tíí!híí	high	'bamboo'	CVV!CVV
f. ?ì!tì	low	'forehead'	CV!CV
g. tì!?í	low-high	'honey bee'	CV!CV
h. tí!hì	high-low	'tobacco'	CV!CV

Table 4: Tone independent of stress

2. Procedure

As noted in the preceding section, stress and tone are independent processes in Pirahã. Based on Everett and Everett's (1984) impressionistic study of the prosody of the language, stress is realized by an increase in amplitude but not fundamental frequency. This section describes the experimental procedures that were used to determine the acoustic correlates of stress in Pirahã.

2.1. Experimental design and data

The data for this study were collected in the summers of 1995 and 1996 in a joint effort with Peter Ladefoged, Department of Linguistics, UCLA, and Dan Everett, Department of Linguistics, University of Pittsburgh. The data was recorded from 12 Pirahã speakers, six male and six female. All 12 speakers were monolingual.

As noted earlier, syllable onsets influence the assignment of stress. Thus, pairs of words which contrast minimally for one consonant position, were selected for the study. Two pairs of the words which were chosen and recorded for this experiment can be seen in Table 5. These four words were recorded in a natural utterance. It was not possible to find a single sentential frame for the four words which the Pirahã speakers would accept. As a result, these four words were collected in four separate sentential frames. Table 5 also contains the sentential frames.

Token	*Sentence*		*Gloss*
!kàbà	?í-!kàbà		
	animal/classifier-gone		'The meat is gone.'
gà!bà	?àò-!?ààgá	gà!bà	
	there-to be	jacamar	'There are jacamar.'
!pìgì	!pìgì	kói	
	swift	really	'It is really swift.'
bò!gì	?í-bò!gì	?àò-!?ààgá	
	her-chest	there-to be	'She has milk.'

Table 5: Four tokens and sentences

These four tokens were chosen from a list of 18 tokens that were recorded and measured for this study. Since these four tokens are the most controlled words for illustrating stress changes, they were chosen for the statistical analysis presented in this paper. See Appendix 1 for the complete list of tokens with their frames, and Appendix 2 for all measurements.

The recordings were done on a Sony DAT, using a close-talking, noise-canceling head mounted microphone so that it was possible to maintain a 45 dB signal/noise ratio.

2.2. Data analysis

The recorded speech was digitized at a sampling rate of 16 kHz, using XWAVES, an interactive graphics interface to the Entropic Signal Processing System (ESPS) on a Sun 4/80 (SPARCstation 10). The research was conducted at the Linguistics Laboratory, Department of Linguistics, University of Pittsburgh.

The data were analyzed with a two-factor analysis of variance (ANOVA) testing for the significant effects of stress and position in the word, on the acoustic properties of the stressed and unstressed syllables in the four tokens under investigation noted in Table 5 above.

3. Results

This section presents the results of a quantitative study of the acoustic correlates of stress, examining specifically the amplitude, duration, fundamental frequency (F0) and formant frequencies of stressed and unstressed syllables considered in light of the reported acoustic correlates of stress in stress-accent languages, pitch-accent languages and tone languages. The question asked is, "How does Pirahã's use of acoustic correlates for stress compare to their use in stress-accent, pitch-accent and other tone languages?"

3.1. Amplitude

It has been shown that increased amplitude of the nucleus of a syllable is an acoustic correlate of stress in many languages. This is especially true for stress languages such as English (Lieberman 1960, Lea 1977, Fry 1955, Beckman 1986), German and French (Fry 1968). But there are stress languages such as Estonian where greater amplitude is not a consistent correlate of stress (Lehiste 1968a). Amplitude is not a significant acoustic correlate for pitch-accent languages such as Japanese (Oyakawa 1971, Mitsuya and Sugito 1963, Weitzman 1969, Beckman 1986), Serbo-Croatian (Lehiste and Ivic 1986) and Norwegian (Swadesh 1937). While F0 is usually the primary acoustic correlate for accent in pitch-accent languages, greater amplitude may also be used as a secondary correlate, as is the case in Swedish (Malmberg 1956). The two tone languages of Diuxi Mixtec (Pike 1976) and Maya (Pike 1946) use intensity as the main acoustic correlate for stress. Since amplitude behaves differently with respect to stressed vowels for these different language types, the amplitude of vowels for stressed and unstressed vowels was measured in Pirahã to see how this acoustic correlate behaves with respect to stress.

3.1.1. Procedure

Amplitude was measured for stressed and unstressed syllables at the point in the vowel at which amplitude was greatest. Figure 2 shows two words which illustrate stress contrasts, one with stress on the first syllable, /!kàbà/ 'not', and the other with stress on the second syllable, /gà!bà/, 'jacamar'. Amplitude measurements are shown for these two words on amplitude displays, which are aligned with the waveform display for the same words.

The power tool used here computes the mean of the squared values for amplitude and plots a graph. These power values are not converted into decibels.

3.1.2. Results

The vowels of stressed syllables have a significantly greater amplitude than the vowels of the unstressed syllables ($F[1,284]=49.12$, $p<.0001$).

	Mean	*St.Dev.*	*n*	*F-value*	*P-value*
stressed	6.0	3.9	143	49.119	.0001
unstressed	3.3	2.2	145		

Table 6. Mean amplitude of vowels in stressed and unstressed syllables.

/!kàbà/ 'not'

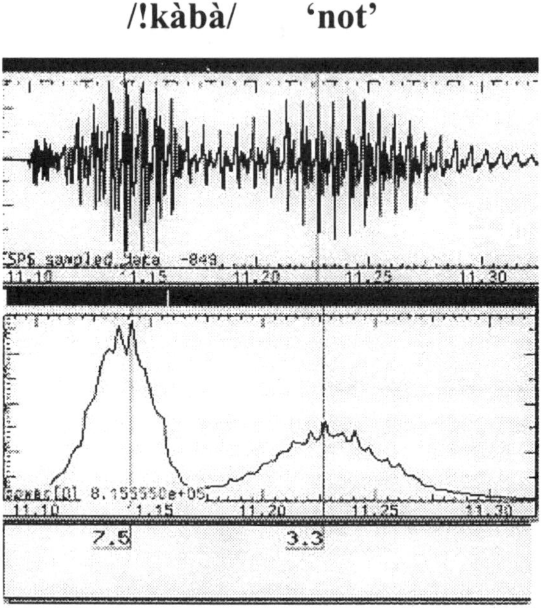

/gà!bà/ 'Jacamar'

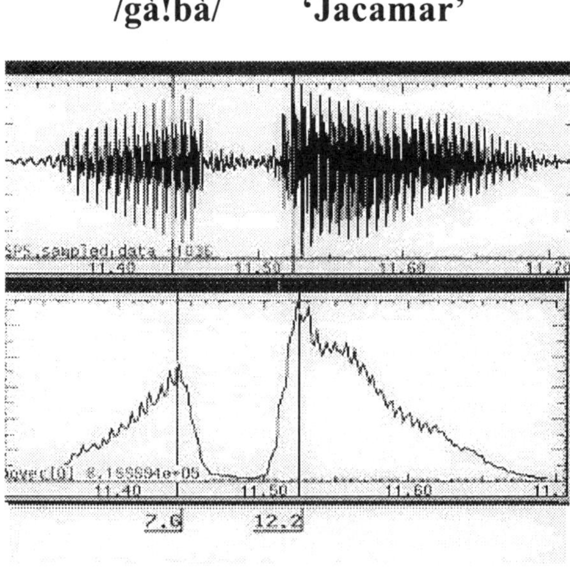

Figure 2

3.1.3 Discussion

Amplitude is a highly significant correlate of stress in Pirahã. The amplitude of stressed syllables is almost twice that of unstressed syllables in Pirahã. Since it has been established that the minimally noticeable difference of an overall amplitude between syllables is approximately 12% , about 1dB (Flanagan 1957), it is clear that the amplitude difference in Pirahã is significant. English, a stress-accent system, also uses amplitude as one of its main acoustic correlates, but unlike Pirahã, the stressed and unstressed syllables of English only become well separated for amplitude when the integral of the energy within the vowel is calculated (Lehto 1971; Medress, Skinner, and Anderson 1971, Beckman 1986, Lieberman 1960). For Pirahã, measuring the maximum intensity of the vowel was sufficient to maintain a highly significant separation in amplitude for stressed and unstressed positions. Another observation that needs to be made here which makes Pirahã distinct from stress-accent systems and pitch-accent systems is that amplitude does not favor high pitch. Both high and low tones are equally amplified when in stressed positions. For example, for these minimally contrasting words for tone, !tígí 'saracura', and !tìgì 'hard' amplitude patterns are the same. Also, Pirahã is distinct from pitch-accent languages like Japanese (Beckman 1986) and Serbocroatian (Lehiste and Ivic ′ 1963), since these do not use amplitude as a dominant correlate of stress. Huang (1969) notes for Chinese, a tone language, that unstressed syllables are not spoken with the intensity of stressed syllables. Pirahã's use of amplitude is most like the tone languages of Diuxi (Pike 1976) and Maya (Pike 1946), in which stress is mainly intensity.

3.2. Duration

Duration has been shown to be an important acoustic correlate of stress in many languages. It is reported to be the second most important acoustic correlate, after F0 for English (Fry 1955; 1958, Mol and Uhlenbeck 1956, Bolinger 1958, Denes and Pinson 1963). Bolinger (1958) regarded vowel duration in English as a covariable with the use of high pitch for marking stressed syllables. Lehiste (1970) reports that in many European languages duration is one of the acoustic correlates of stress. While several investigators have shown that vowel length is not a consistent correlate of stress in Japanese (Oyakawa 1971, Mitsuya and Sugito 1978, Beckman 1986), others have shown that accented syllables in Japanese have greater length (Wenck 1966). In Serbo-Croatian, another pitch-accent language, accented vowels are considerably longer than unstressed vowels (Lehiste and Ivic ‵ 1986). Finally, duration is an acoustic correlate of stress in the tone languages of Marinahua (Pike and Scott 1962), Siane (Lucht and James 1962), Diuxi Mixtec (Pike 1974), Maya (Pike 1946) and Chinese (Huang 1969). The duration of vowels and consonants of stressed and unstressed syllables were measured to see how this acoustic correlate behaves with respect to stress in Pirahã.

3.2.1. Procedure

Three durations were measured: duration of the vowels of stressed and unstressed syllables in penultimate and final positions, duration of the intervocalic consonantal onset of the final stressed and unstressed syllables, and the total duration of the stressed and unstressed syllables in final position. The durations of vowels in stressed and unstressed positions were measured from the onset to the offset of the first three formants of the vowels. The duration of the onsets of the second syllables were measured from the offset to the onset of formant structures of the vowels on either side of the consonants. Finally, the duration of the final syllable is the cumulative durations of the intervocalic consonant and final vowel. Figure 3 on the next page gives wideband spectrograms with time-aligned waveforms showing how the consonants and vowels were measured.

3.2.2. Results

Duration of stressed and unstressed vowels

The vowels of unstressed syllables have a significantly greater duration than the vowels of stressed syllables (F[1,139]=12.502, p=.0005).

	Mean	*St.Dev.*	*n*	*F-value*	*P-value*
stressed	85	22	143	12.502	.0005
unstressed	93	22	145		

Table 7: Mean duration of vowels in stressed and unstressed syllables

Duration of final syllables

In the case of final syllables, the cumulative duration of the stressed syllables is significantly greater than unstressed syllables (F[1,139]=14.811, p=.0002). In final position the initial consonant of the stressed syllable is 27 ms greater in duration than the corresponding consonant in the unstressed syllable. The mean duration of the vowels of the unstressed final syllable, however, is 9 ms greater than the vowels of the stressed syllable. The difference in duration of the vowels is not as great as the difference in duration of the initial consonants. Consequently, the cumulative duration of the stressed syllable is greater than the cumulative duration of the unstressed syllable in final position.

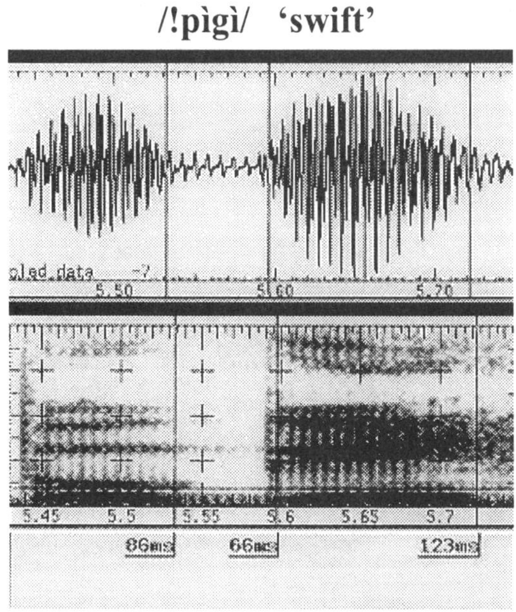
/!pìgì/ 'swift'
5.50
5.70
5.45
5.5
5.55
5.65
5.7
86ms
66ms
123ms

/bò!gì/ 'chest'

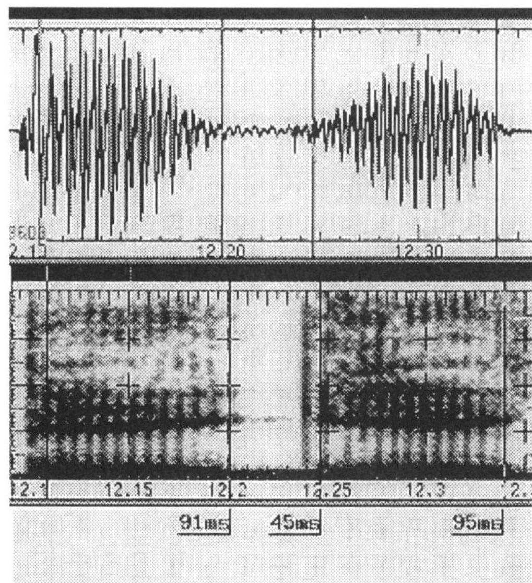
12.20
12.30
12.15
12.3
91ms
45ms
95ms

Figure 3

	Mean	*St.Dev.*	*n*	*F-value*	*P-value*
stressed	71	16	71	148.325	.0001
unstressed	44	11	72		

Table 8: Mean duration of onset consonants in stressed and unstressed syllables in final position.

	Mean	*St.Dev.*	*n*	*F-value*	*P-value*
stressed	91	25	71	6.162	.0142
unstressed	100	18	72		

Table 9: Mean duration of vowels in stressed and unstressed syllables in final position.

	Mean	*St.Dev.*	*n*	*F-value*	*P-value*
stressed	161	35	71	14.811	.0002
unstressed	143	22	72		

Table 10: Mean duration of stressed and unstressed syllables in final position.

3.2.3. Discussion

Increased duration is an acoustic correlate of stress in Pirahã. However, the increase in duration is not due to an increase in the vowel length. Stressed vowels are significantly shorter than unstressed. This contrasts with English and other European languages where length in stressed positions is carried mainly on the vowel. There are, however, other languages where the use of duration for distinguishing the stressed and unstressed positions is not done by vowel lengthening of the stressed vowel. Of special interest is the relation of stress and length in Estonian, a stress-accent language. There are three contrasting syllable lengths and these do not change their length when stressed. But there is a negative correlation of stress and length in that unstressed syllables are shortened (Raun and Saareste 1965). Fónogy (1966) reports that many unstressed vowels are regularly longer than stressed vowels for Hungarian. The exact behavior of vowel length with respect to stress is quite varied depending on the language.

Fry (1968) makes the general statement that stressed syllables regularly contain vowels of greater length than of corresponding unstressed syllables. For Pirahã this would need to be modified to include onsets in duration measurements as it is only when onsets are include that the stressed syllable is significantly longer than the unstressed syllable. Note, although it is not necessary to include syllable onsets in Enligh to establish stressed syllables as longer than unstressed syllables, it is nontheless the case that stops have longer duration before a stressed vowel than before an unstressed vowel (Malecot 1968).

3.3. Fundamental Frequency

The most important acoustic correlate to be measured and discussed in this paper is fundamental frequency because of the ambiguity that arises due to its double use as a dominant correlate of stress and primary correlate of tone (See Section 1.2.). First, fundamental frequency is understood to be the dominant correlate of stress in stress-accent languages such as English (Liebrman 1960, Fry 1955; 1958, Mol and Uhlenbeck 1956, Bolinger 1958, Hyman 1978), Polish (Jassem 1959) and French (Rigault 1962). It is also a dominant acoustic correlate of accent for the pitch-accent languages such as Japanese (Beckman 1986), Serbo-Croatian (Lehiste and Ivic ' 1986), Swedish (Malmberg 1940) and Norwegian (Swadesh 1937). The second use of F0 is as the principle correlate of tone for all tone languages (Pike 1948). In order to better understand how this double use of F0 is handled in Pirahã, F0 was measured for stressed and unstressed vowels, specifically noting the behavior of lexical tones in these positions.

3.3.1. Procedure

The fundamental frequency of stressed and unstressed syllables was taken at the point of greatest amplitude in the vowel. Figure 4 on the next page shows two contrasting words for stress placement, /!kàbà/ 'not', and / gà!bà/ 'jacamar' with time-aligned F0 and amplitude displays. The vertical lines in the displays indicate where F0 measurements were recorded.

3.3.2. Results

The F0 of the vowels of stressed syllables is not significantly different from the F0 of the vowels of the unstressed syllables.

	Mean	*St.Dev.*	*n*	*F-value*	*P-value*
stressed	185	45	143	.586	.4446
unstressed	181	45	145		

Table 11: Mean F0 of vowels in stressed and unstressed syllables.

3.3.3. Discussion

While F0 is a major correlate of stress in both stress-accent and pitch-accent languages, this is not the case for Pirahã. Pirahã shows no significant

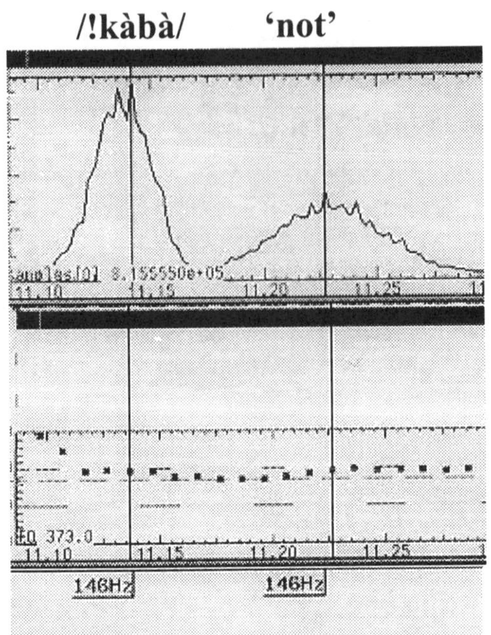
/!kàbà/ 'not'
11.10
11.15
11.20
11.25
F0 373.0
11.10
11.15
11.20
11.25
146Hz
146Hz

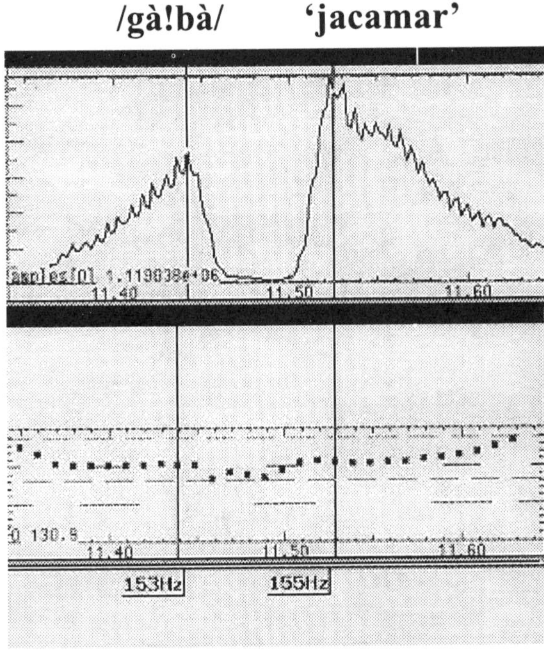
/gà!bà/ 'jacamar'
11.40
11.50
11.60
130.9
11.40
11.50
11.60
153Hz
155Hz

Figure 4

changes in F0 for stressed and unstressed positions. This contrasts with the stress-accent language of Estonian in which a rise in pitch characterizes the stressed syllable as distinct from the unstressed syllable (Raun and Saareste 1965). In Swedish, a pitch accent language, high pitch occurs on the stressed syllable (Hadding-Koch 1961). In Japanese, another pitch-accent language, high pitch occurs on stressed syllables (Wenck 1966). It is important to note that the use of F0 to indicate stress in stress-accent and pitch-accent languages is done mainly through the use of high pitch. Fry (1968:373) observes that there is a definite tendency for high relative pitch to carry an implication of greater stress. He extends this generalization to tone languages because, he notes, in a tone language a higher variant of a tone occurs when the syllable bearing the tone is stressed. Fry's inclusion of tone languages for this general tendency needs to be more carefully examined. The tone languages observed for this study showed no such tendency. It certainly is not the case for Pirahã, where contrasting high and low tones remain unchanged for F0 for stressed positions. And for all other tone languages observed for this study, there was no instance of contrasting tones favoring a higher pitch allotone when stressed. For example, in Chinese when a syllable is stressed a high tone become higher, a low tone becomes lower and the pitch range of contours become more exaggerated (Chao 1968, Xiao-nan 1984, Howie 1976, Tseng 1981). According to Pike (1948) the correlation between high pitch and stress, as seen in stress-accent languages, does not occur in tone languages. (See 4.2 for further discussion.)

3.4. Formant frequency

Fry (1968) states that there is almost a universal tendency for vowel quality to be more open and more central in weaker syllables than in stressed ones. For English (Lindblom 1963, Tiffany 1959), British English (Holmes 1962), French (Fry 1968), Russian (Avanesov 1956), and Estonian (Lehiste 1964a) the set of vowels for unstressed positions is smaller than the set of vowels for stressed positions, partially due to this universal tendency. In Swedish (Lehiste 1970, Lindblom 1963, Fant 1962) and Serbo-Croatian (Lehiste and Ivic' 1986), pitch-accent languages, there is also vowel reduction in unstressed positions. Wenck (1966) explains that for Japanese, another pitch accent language, certain reduced syllables cannot carry stress. Since vowel quality is understood to be one of the possible acoustic correlates of stress in the world's languages, the values of the first and second formants, F1 and F2, were measured for stressed and unstressed vowels in Pirahã.

3.4.1. Procedure

The following 4 disyllabic tokens, presented in Table 5, were chosen to measure formants one and two in stressed and unstressed positions.

1. !kà'bà	'not'
2. gà!bà'	'jacamar'
3. !pì'gì	'swift'
5. !tí'gí	'hard'

Table 12. Vowel quality and stress

Frequencies for the first and second formants were measured for stressed and unstressed vowels in these words to determine if there were any quality changes associated with stress.

Figure 5 illustrates a wideband spectrogram, aligned with a waveform for the word /gà!bà/ 'jacamar', showing where measurements were taken for formants one and two of each vowel. Measurements were made at the most steady point of the vowel.

gà!bà 'jacamar'

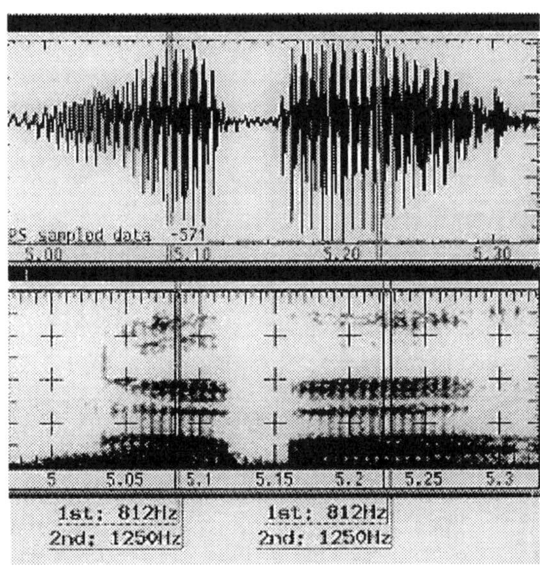

Figure 5

	Formant 1	*Formant 2*
Formant readings for first syllable	812Hz	1250Hz
Formant readings for the second syllable	812Hz	1250Hz

3.4.2. Results

The formant frequencies of F1 and F2 for the vowels of stressed syllables are not significantly different from the formant frequencies of the vowels of the unstressed syllables.

	Mean	*St.Dev.*	*n*	*F-value*	*P-value*
F1, stressed [a]	851	124	24	.002	.9644
F1, unstressed [a]	853	105	24		
F2, stressed [a]	1528	259	24	.533	.4694
F2, unstressed [a]	1578	261	24		
F1, stressed [i]	344	33	12	.000	.9957
F1, unstressed [i]	343	42	12		
F2, stressed [i]	2469	193	12	.790	.3838
F2, unstressed [i]	2541	209	12		

Table 13. Mean formant frequencies for F1 and F2 of the vowels [a] and [i] in stressed and unstressed syllables

3.4.3. Discussion

For this set of words it is clear that in Pirahã stress does not interact with vowel quality. Pike (1974) reports that the type of vowel quality changes that occur when high pitch accompanies stress in stress-accent and pitch-accent languages, are not as common for tone languages. Also, it is not likely that there would be a smaller set of vowels for unstressed positions in Pirahã since it already has a small inventory of vowels.

3.5. Summary

The primary acoustic correlates of stress in Pirahã are amplitude and duration. The vowels of stressed syllables have significantly greater amplitude. In addition, stressed syllables have a significantly greater duration. The greater duration of stressed syllables is the result of the greater duration of the onsets of stressed syllables. Finally, the F0 and formant frequencies of F1 and F2 were not significantly different in the vowels of the stressed and unstressed syllables.

When comparing the behavior of the acoustic correlates of stress in Pirahã with the behavior of the same in stress and pitch-accent languages, there are a few clear observations to be made. First, it uses amplitude as do most stress-accent systems, although its use of amplitude is more significant than that observed for the stress-accent systems in that the integral of the energy within the vowel does not need to be considered to establish significant differences in amplitude for stressed and unstressed vowels. Second, Pirahã uses duration differently than stress-accent languages such as English where higher pitch and longer vowels tend to be covariants for stress. Third, F0 is not used to indicate stress as is the case for stress-accent and pitch-accent languages. And the final observation to be made is that vowel quality is not an indicator of stress in Pirahã as it is for most stress-accent and pitch-accent systems looked at in this study.

4. Conclusion

The results from this study document a language, Pirahã, in which the phonetics of stress are amplitude and duration. The important theoretical issues raised by Pirahã facts are that lexical tone and predictable stress co-occur, and stress does not use F0. These facts raise further questions not only as to possible phonetic typologies of stress but also as to possible phonetic typologies of tone for tone languages.

4.1. Further research on the phonetics of stress

Most phonetic typologies of stress have the underlying presupposition that the phonetics of stress are dependent on F0 (See 1.2.). Pirahã presents a language whose phonetics of stress are amplitude and duration. Diuxi, another tone language, whose phonetics of stress are intensity and duration, also does not use F0 for stress (Pike 1976). While there are many clear examples of stress-accent languages and pitch-accent languages where pitch, more specifically, high pitch, is strongly linked to stress, there are also examples, such as Pirahã and Diuxi, where the phonetics of stress may have combinations of acoustic correlates that do not include F0. More acoustical studies need to be done specifically of tone languages, investigating the behavior of F0 with respect to stress and tone, looking to see if there might be a combination of phonetic correlates of stress for tone languages that is different from the phonetics of stress for non-tone languages.

4.2. Further research on the phonetics of tone

Because Pirahã is a tone language which also has predictable stress that does not use F0, it not only permits a close examination of what stress looks like phonetically in a situation where F0 is not used, but it also permits a more controlled look at the phonetics of tone. Pirahã's tone system, like other tone languages, is not only distinct from stress in its function, but the behavior of F0 for tone when stressed is different from the behavior of F0 when it is used as the main acoustic correlate of stress in stress and pitch-accent languages (Pike, 1948). Not only does F0, when used to indicate stress, have a very high occurrence with high pitch within the stressed syllable, there is also a set of possible segment changes that accompany the use of F0 as an acoustic correlate of stress that does not occur when F0 is used for lexical tone in a tone language. When F0 is used as an acoustic correlate of stress, there is a dominant use of higher pitch in connection with greater amplitude, greater vowel length and a larger set of vowels. High pitch holds no such privileged spot in tone languages. As noted by Schuh (1986), tones in a tone language, whether they are high, mid, low or contour, tend to undergo predictable changes themselves when stressed. Further quantitative, acoustical studies of the behavior of F0 in tone languages need to be done to help untangle the behavior of F0 as a dominate acoustic correlate of stress from its use for lexical tone in tone languages.

References

Ariste, P. 1939. A quantitative language. Proceedings of the third international congress of phonetic sciences. 276-80.

Avanesov, R.I. 1956. Fonetika sovremennogo russkogo literaturenogo jazyka. Moscow: University of Moscow.

Beckman, Mary. 1986. Stress and non-stress accent. Dordrecht: Foris.

Bloomfield, Leonard. 1933. Language. Holt, Rinehart and Winston.

Bolinger, Dwight L. 1958. Word 14:109-149.

Chao, Y.R. 1968. A grammar of spoken Chinese. Berkeley: University of California Press.

Duanmu, S. 1990. A formal study of syllable, tone stress and domain in Chinese languages. Ph.D. dissertation, Massachusetts Institute of Technology.

_______. 1996. Tone: an overview. Glot International 2, no. 4.

Edmundson, T., and J. T. Bendor Samuel. 1966. Tone patterns of Etung. Journal of African Languages 5:1-6.

Everett, Daniel L. 1979. Aspectos da fonologia do Pirahã. M.A. thesis, Universidade Estadual de Campinas.

_______. 1986. Pirahã. Handbook of Amazonian Languages I, ed. Desmond Derbyshire and Geoffrey Pullum, pp. 200-326. Berlin: Mouton de Gruyter.

_______. 1988. On metrical constituent structure in Pirahã, phonology. Natural language and linguistic theory 6: 207-246.

Everett, Keren. 1978. Phonological prerequisites in Pirahã (ms.).

Everett, Daniel L. and Keren Everett. 1984. On the relevance of syllable onsets and stress placement. Linguistic Inquiry 15:705-711.

Fant, Gunner. 1962. Den Akustika fonetikens grunder. Kungl.Tek. Hogskol., Taltransmissionslab. 2nd printing. Stockholm: Royal Institute of Technology, no. 7

Flanagan, J. L. 1957. Estimates of the maximum precision necessary in quantizing certain "dimensions" of vowel sounds. Journal of the Acoustical Society of America 28:533-534.

Fónogy, Ivan. 1966. Electrophysical and acoustic correlates of stress and stress perception. Journal of speech and hearing research 9:231-244.

Fromkin, Victoria A. 1978. Tone: a linguistic survey. Academic Press: New York.

Fry, Dennis. 1955. Duration and intensity as physical correlates of linguistic stress. Journal of Acoustical Society of America 27:765-768.

_______. 1958. Experiments in the perception of stress. Language and Speech 1:126-152.

_______. 1965. The dependence of stress judgments on vowel formant structure. Proceedings of the Fifth International Congress of Phonetic Sciences, pp. 306-311.

_______. 1968. Prosodic phenomena. Manual of Phonetics, ed. B. Malmberg. Amsterdam: North Holland Publishing Company.

Goldsmith, J. 1976. Autosegmental phonology. Ph.D. dissertation, Massachusetts Institute of Technology. [Reproduced by the Indiana University Linguistics Club, Bloomington, Indiana.]

_______. 1981. English as a tone language. Phonology in the 1980's, ed. D. L. Goyvaerts pp. 287-308. Ghent, Belgium: E. Story-Scientia.

_______. 1982. Accent systems. The structure of phonological representations (Part I), ed. H. van der Hulst & N. Smith, pp. 47-63. [Linguistic Models, 2]. Dordrecht: Foris.

Hadding-Kock, Kerstin. 1961. Acoustical-phonetic studies in the intonation of Southern Swedish. Trav. Inst. Phon. Lund III.

Howie, John Marshall. 1976. Acoustical studies of Mandarin vowels and tones. Cambridge: Cambridge University Press.

Huang, Raymond. 1969. Mandarin Pronunciation. Hong Kong: Hong Kong University Press.

Hyman, Larry. 1978. Tone and/or accent. Elements of tone, stress and intonation, ed. J. Napoli, pp. 1-19. Washington: Georgetown University Press.

Jassem, Wiktor. 1959. The phonology of Polish stress. Word 15:252-269.

Kingdon, Roger. 1958a. The groundwork for English Intonation. Longmans, Green and Co.

________. 1958b. The groundwork for English Stress. Longmans, Green and Co.

Lea, W. A. 1973a. Syntactic boundaries and stress patterns in spoken English. Univac Report No. PX 10146. St. Paul, Minnesota: Sperry Univac DSD.

_______. 1973b. Segmental and Suprasegmental Influences on Fundamental Frequency Contours. Consonant types and tone (Proceedings of the First Annual Southern California Round Table in Linguistics), ed. L. Hyman. Los Angeles: University of Southern California Press.

_______. 1977. Acoustic correlates of stress and juncture. Studies in stress and accent, ed. L. Hyman. Southern California occasional papers in linguistics 4.

Leben, William. 1973. Suprasegmental phonology. Ph.D. dissertation, Massachusetts Institute of Technology.

Lehiste, Ilse. 1964. Compounding as a phonological process. Proceedings of the 9th International Congress of Linguistics. The Hague: Mouton & Co., 331-337.

_______. 1970. Suprasegmentals. Cambridge: MIT Press.

Lieberman, P. 1960. Some acoustic correlates of word stress in American English. Journal of the Acoustic Society of America 32:451-454.

Lindblom, B. 1963. Spectrographic study of vowel reduction. Journal of the acoustical society of America 35: 1173-1781.

Malmberg, Bertil. 1940. Recherches experimentales sur l'accent musical du mot en Suedois. Archives Neerlandaises de phonetique experimentale 13:129-37.

________. 1956. Questions de methode en phonetique synchronique. Stud. Ling. 10:1.

Mitsuya, Fumiko and Miyoko Sugito. 1978. A study of the accentual effect on segmental and moraic duration in Japanese. Annual bulletin of the Research Institute of Logopedics and Phoniatrics 12: 97-112. Tokyo: University of Tokyo.

Medress, M. F., D. E. Skinner, and Anderson. 1972. Acoustic correlates of word stress. Journal of the Acoustical Society of America 72, 101. The 82nd meeting of the Acoustical Society of America.

Mol, H. and E. M. Uhlenbeck. 1956. The linguistic relevance of intensity in stress. Lingua 5:205-213.

Napoli, Donna Jo. 1978. Elements of tone, stress, and intonation. Georgetown University.

Oyakawa, Takatsugu. 1971. On the duration of Japanese short vowels. Monthly internal memorandum, Linguistics Department. Berkeley: University of California.

van der Hulst, H. & N. Smith. (eds.) 1988. Autosegmental studies on pitch-accent. (Linguistic Models) 17. Berlin: Mouton de Gruyter.

Pike, Eunice V. 1974. A multiple stress system versus a tone system. International journal of American linguistics 40:169-175.

_______. 1976. Stress and tone in the phonology of Diuxi Mixtec. Phonetica 33:321-333.

Pike, Kenneth L. 1946. Phonemic Pitch in Maya. International journal of American linguistics 12:82-88.

_______. 1948. Tone languages. Ann Arbor:University of Michigan Press.

Pulleyblank, D. 1983. Tone in lexical Phonology. Ph.D. dissertation, Massachusetts Institute of Technology.

Raun, Alo and Andrus Saareste. 1965. Introduction to Estonian Linguistics. Wiesbaden: Otto Harrassowitz.

Rigault, A. 1962. Role de la frequence, de l'intensite et de la duree vocaliques dans la perception de l'accent en francais. Proc. 4th Int. Congre. Phonet. Sci. p. 735. The Hague.

Shearme, J.N. and J.N. Holmes. 1962. An experimental study of the classification of sounds in continuous speech according to their distribution in the formant 1-formant 2 plan. Proceedings of the 4th International Congress of Phonetic Sciences. pp. 234-240. The Hague: Mouton & Co.

Schuh, Russell G. 1978. Tone rules. Tone: a linguistic survey, Victoria Fromkin. Academic Press.

Swadesh, Morris. 1937. The phonemic interpretation of long consonants. Language 13:1-10.

Tiffany, W.R. 1959. Non-random sources of variation in vowel quality. Journal of speech and hearing research 2: 305-317.

Trager, George L., and Henry Lee Smith. 1951. An outline of English structure. Battenburg Press.

Tseng, Chiu-yu. 1981. An acoustic study on tones in Mandarin Chinese. Ph.D. dissertation, Brown University.

Weitzman, Raymond S. 1969. Japanese accent: an analysis based on acoustic-phonetic data. Ph.D. dissertation, University of Southern California.

Wenck, Gunther. 1966. The phonemics of Japanese - questions and attempts. Wiesbaden: Otto Harrassowitz.

Williams, E. 1976. Underlying tone in Margi and Igbo. Linguistic Inquiry 7:436-468.

Appendix 1

The following is a list of the sentences that were used to collect the tokens used for this study.

1. ?í-!<u>kàbà</u>
   animal/classifier-gone
   'The meat is gone.' [The prefix ?í- cannot receive stress]

2. ?àò-!?ààgá <u>gà!bà</u>
   there/pron.-to be/temporary jacamar
   'There are jacamar.'

3. !<u>pìgì</u> kóì
   swift really
   'It is really swift.'

4. ?í-<u>bò!gì</u> ?àò-!?ààgá-há
   her/pron.-milk there/pron.-to be/temporary-declarative
   'The woman has milk.' [The prefix ?í- cannot receive stress]

5. !<u>tígí</u> kòòhòì !?áàgà-há
   saracura nest is-declarative
   'It is a saracura nest.'

6. tòò!tòò !?áàgà-há
duck to be/permanent-declarative
'It is a duck.'

7. !tì'gì kói
hard really
'It is really hard.'

8. ?í-!sàbí
animal/classifier-mean
'The animal is mean.' [The prefix ?í- cannot receive stress]

9. bì!gí kàò bí
ground fall
'It just now fell.'

10. gí!?à ?òò-!íìga bòò!tóì' !?áàgà-hà
you hand-back scar to be/permanent-declarative
'You have a scar on the back of your hand.'

11. pì!káágíhí ?àò-!?ààgá-há
goddess of the river there-to be/temporary-declarative
'Pìkáágìhì exists.'

Note: For token 11, the antipenult and penult syllables are compared for measurement.

12. pì!káá'gíhí ?àò-!?àà'gá-há
goddess of the river there/pron.-to be/temporary-declarative
'Pìkáágìhì exists.'

Note: For token 12, the antepenult and the final syllables are compared for measurement.

13. ?í!sì ?àò-!?ààgá-há
meat there/pron.-to be/temporary-declarative
'There is meat.'

14. ?àò-!?ààgá-há tò!bàì
there/pron.-to be/temporary-declarative sorva
'There is sorva.'

15. ?àpà-!pà !gáìgá-hóíhàì
head-reflexive tie-future tense
'You will tie your head.' [The suffix hóíhàì cannot receive stress]

Note: for token 15, antepenult and final syllables are compared for measurement.

16. ?àpà-!pà !gáìgá-hóíhàì
head-reflexive tie-future tense
'You will tie your head.'

Note: for token 16, the penult and final syllables are compared for measurement.

17. !pìì?ìhì ?í-!sàíbáhá
    Juruti animal/classifier-a lot
    'There are a lot of Juruti.

Note: for token 17 the antepenult and penult syllables are compared for measurement.

18. !pìì?ìhì ?í-!sàíbáhá
    Juruti animal/classifier-a lot
    'There are a lot of Juruti.'

Note: for token 18 the antepenult and final syllables are compared for measurement.

Appendix 2

This appendix contains two sections. The first section contains all the measurements for vowel amplitude, frequency, duration and formant frequencies. Duration and formant frequencies are not included for all tokens. The second section contains consonant measurements.

Section 1: All vowel measurements

Interpretation of columns:

tok(ens): 1=!kàbà 'not'

1a=first repetition

1b=second repetition

2=gà!bà 'jacamar'

2a=first repetition

2b=second repetition

3=!pìgì 'swift'

3a=first repetition

3b=second repetition

4=bò!gì 'chest'

4a=first repetition

4b=second repetition

5=!tí'gí 'saracura'

5a=first repetition

5b=second repetition

6=tòò!tòò 'duck'

7=!tìgì 'hard'

7a=first repetition

7b=second repetition

8=!sàbí 'mean'

9=bì!gí 'ground'

10=gí!?à 'your'

11=(pì)!káágí(hí) 'small fish'

12=(pì)!káá(gí)hí 'small fish'

13=?í!sì 'meat'

14=tò!bàì 'sorva' (tree rubber)

15=?à(pà)!pà 'head reflexive'

16=(?a)pà!pà 'head reflexive'

17=!pìì?ì(hì) 'juruti' (a type of bird)

18=!pìì(?ì)hì 'juruti' (a type of bird)

sub(ject): speaker number

sex: 1=male

2=female

amp(litude): measurement for power of the vowel, (the power number is the mean of the squared values of amplitude)

vow(el): a

i

o

aa

ii

oo

a

tone: 1=high tone

2=low tone

syl(lable): antip(enult)

penult

final

str(ess): 1=stressed
2=unstressed
freq(uency): measurments in Hz for vowel
dur(ation): measurements in milliseconds for vowel
for1: measurements in Hz for first formant
for2: measurements in Hz for second formant
for3: measurements in Hz for third formant.

sub	sex	tok	amp	vow	tone	syl	str	freq	vdur	for1	for2	for3
1	1	1	12.0	a	2	penult	1	150	82			
2	1	1	4.7	a	2	penult	1	125	86			
3	1	1	3.4	a	2	penult	1	144	78			
4	1	1	2.4	a	2	penult	1	126	96			
5	1	1	10.0	a	2	penult	1	164	86			
6	1	1	2.5	a	2	penult	1	136	58			
7	2	1	7.1	a	2	penult	1	260	64			
8	2	1	4.0	a	2	penult	1	235	68			
9	2	1	4.3	a	2	penult	1	238	78			
10	2	1	1.6	a	2	penult	1	205	78			
11	2	1	2.1	a	2	penult	1	236	94			
12	2	1	4.4	a	2	penult	1	225	42			
1	1	1	9.1	a	2	final	2	149	102			
2	1	1	2.8	a	2	final	2	130	106			
3	1	1	1.0	a	2	final	2	134	108			
4	1	1	1.2	a	2	final	2	129	116			
5	1	1	5.8	a	2	final	2	165	108			
6	1	1	2.0	a	2	final	2	131	77			
7	2	1	3.1	a	2	final	2	148	113			
8	2	1	3.3	a	2	final	2	126	86			
9	2	1	3.5	a	2	final	2	233	112			

sub	sex	tok	amp	vow	tone	syl	str	freq	vdur
10	2	1	1.3	a	2	final	2	196	108
11	2	1	1.7	a	2	final	2	236	117
12	2	1	3.6	a	2	final	2	229	74
1	1	la	13.0	a	2	penult	1	148	66
2	1	la	3.3	a	2	penult	1	121	56
3	1	la	3.6	a	2	penult	1	151	70
4	1	la	14.0	a	2	penult	1	120	82
5	1	la	4.7	a	2	penult	1	167	67
6	1	la	2.8	a	2	penult	1	133	63
7	2	la	13.0	a	2	penult	1	263	90
8	2	la	4.0	a	2	penult	1	230	80
9	2	la	2.3	a	2	penult	1	232	78
10	2	la	14.0	a	2	penult	1	202	78
11	2	la	2.1	a	2	penult	1	236	96
12	2	la	6.6	a	2	penult	1	212	92
1	1	la	8.0	a	2	final	2	150	70
2	1	la	1.2	a	2	final	2	122	67
3	1	la	1.1	a	2	final	2	142	94
4	1	la	5.1	a	2	final	2	121	120
5	1	la	2.1	a	2	final	2	165	78
6	1	la	1.9	a	2	final	2	133	84
7	2	la	9.0	a	2	final	2	256	102
8	2	la	1.7	a	2	final	2	230	86
9	2	la	1.8	a	2	final	2	237	114
10	2	la	9.8	a	2	final	2	202	98
11	2	la	1.7	a	2	final	2	231	110
12	2	la	4.1	a	2	final	2	201	138

sub	sex	tok	amp	vow	tone	syl	str	freq	vdur	for1	for2	for3
1	1	1b	7.3	a	2	penult	1	149	92	750	1250	2375
2	1	1b	6.0	a	2	penult	1	128	95	812	1625	2312
3	1	1b	7.1	a	2	penult	1	150	80	875	1500	2562
4	1	1b	11.1	a	2	penult	1	122	93	786	1500	2500
5	1	1b	6.1	a	2	penult	1	164	82	718	1468	2343
6	1	1b	7.5	a	2	penult	1	147	52	625	1375	2437
7	2	1b	3.3	a	2	penult	1	265	64	812	1625	3312
8	2	1b	2.5	a	2	penult	1	230	62	812	1312	3312
9	2	1b	3.1	a	2	penult	1	231	75	1000	1625	3125
10	2	1b	8.2	a	2	penult	1	258	83	937	1437	3000
11	2	1b	6.0	a	2	penult	1	236	94	875	1625	3187
12	2	1b	6.3	a	2	penult	1	209	46	685	1375	3312
1	1	1b	4.5	a	2	final	2	154	108	750	1250	2437
2	1	1b	4.7	a	2	final	2	127	107	812	1523	2187
3	1	1b	4.9	a	2	final	2	151	96	875	1500	2562
4	1	1b	5.1	a	2	final	2	114	114	786	1500	2500
5	1	1b	3.6	a	2	final	2	164	100	718	1468	2343
6	1	1b	3.2	a	2	final	2	147	73	812	1375	2625
7	2	1b	0.9	a	2	final	2	261	86	812	1750	2937
8	2	1b	1.0	a	2	final	2	232	78	812	1312	3312
9	2	1b	2.2	a	2	final	2	226	110	1000	1625	3125
10	2	1b	3.6	a	2	final	2	251	105	1062	1375	3000
11	2	1b	4.5	a	2	final	2	231	112	875	1625	3187
12	2	1b	2.7	a	2	final	2	207	72	937	1375	3312
1	1	2	4.5	a	2	final	1	146	72			
2	1	2	3.0	a	2	final	1	137	56			
3	1	2	8.2	a	2	final	1	141	86			

sub	sex	tok	amp	vow	tone	syl	str	freq	vdur
4	1	2	2.8	a	2	final	1	133	66
5	1	2	10.0	a	2	final	1	165	58
6	1	2	13.0	a	2	final	1	118	82
7	2	2	14.0	a	2	final	1	243	78
8	2	2	12.0	a	2	final	1	246	78
9	2	2	2.2	a	2	final	1	225	56
10	2	2	2.0	a	2	final	1	214	72
11	2	2	6.0	a	2	final	1	215	98
12	2	2	4.0	a	2	final	1	225	80
1	1	2	3.9	a	2	penult	2	146	108
2	1	2	1.5	a	2	penult	2	131	98
3	1	2	3.1	a	2	penult	2	134	128
4	1	2	1.4	a	2	penult	2	127	103
5	1	2	8.0	a	2	penult	2	156	79
6	1	2	8.0	a	2	penult	2	118	102
7	2	2	8.3	a	2	penult	2	243	120
8	2	2	9.4	a	2	penult	2	242	104
9	2	2	0.9	a	2	penult	2	225	102
10	2	2	1.5	a	2	penult	2	203	106
11	2	2	3.5	a	2	penult	2	207	110
12	2	2	3.0	a	2	penult	2	212	119
1	1	2a	9.7	a	2	final	1	141	74
2	1	2a	12.0	a	2	final	1	137	60
3	1	2a	12.0	a	2	final	1	177	64
4	1	2a	2.4	a	2	final	1	124	90
5	1	2a	3.7	a	2	final	1	160	60
6	1	2a	2.5	a	2	final	1	137	70

sub	sex	tok	amp	vow	tone	syl	str	freq	vdur	for1	for2	for3
7	2	2a	2.3	a	2	final	1	231	84			
8	2	2a	1.5	a	2	final	1	221	74			
9	2	2a	2.0	a	2	final	1	233	72			
10	2	2a	12.0	a	2	final	1	204	62			
11	2	2a	4.6	a	2	final	1	224	102			
12	2	2a	4.3	a	2	final	1	225	96			
1	1	2a	3.6	a	2	penult	2	137	108			
2	1	2a	5.2	a	2	penult	2	131	90			
3	1	2a	7.9	a	2	penult	2	176	90			
4	1	2a	1.0	a	2	penult	2	125	122			
5	1	2a	1.4	a	2	penult	2	158	65			
6	1	2a	1.9	a	2	penult	2	141	110			
7	2	2a	.9	a	2	penult	2	219	132			
8	2	2a	.9	a	2	penult	2	217	85			
9	2	2a	.6	a	2	penult	2	216	110			
10	2	2a	3.0	a	2	penult	2	202	74			
11	2	2a	1.6	a	2	penult	2	222	126			
12	2	2a	3.3	a	2	penult	2	211	174			
1	1	2b	6.6	a	2	final	1	148	125	937	2562	3500
2	1	2b	3.9	a	2	final	1	125	90	812	1625	3687
3	1	2b	6.6	a	2	final	1	141	116	812	1562	4625
4	1	2b	10.1	a	2	final	1	114	110	812	1500	3562
5	1	2b	14.1	a	2	final	1	165	80	1000	1500	3625
6	1	2b	12.1	a	2	final	1	157	104	687	1375	2500
7	2	2b	1.7	a	2	final	1	244	100	875	1750	3437
8	2	2b	8.9	a	2	final	1	220	88	875	1250	2687
9	2	2b	7.4	a	2	final	1	206	100	1000	1250	3312

sub	sex	tok	amp	vow	tone	syl	str	freq	vdur	for1	for2	for3
10	2	2b	2.5	a	2	final	1	226	94	1187	1500	2687
11	2	2b	3.5	a	2	final	1	252	124	812	1562	3062
12	2	2b	2.8	a	2	final	1	206	131	937	1437	3520
1	1	2b	5.6	a	2	penult	2	148	86	1125	2562	3500
2	1	2b	3.1	a	2	penult	2	125	72	812	1625	3697
3	1	2b	5.0	a	2	penult	2	143	86	812	1562	4375
4	1	2b	8.2	a	2	penult	2	120	92	750	1625	3562
5	1	2b	6.4	a	2	penult	2	161	68	870	1500	3525
6	1	2b	6.2	a	2	penult	2	152	72	750	1375	2500
7	2	2b	1.0	a	2	penult	2	237	84	812	1750	3437
8	2	2b	6.2	a	2	penult	2	217	70	1000	1437	2687
9	2	2b	7.4	a	2	penult	2	202	56	812	1937	3812
10	2	2b	1.0	a	2	penult	2	220	78	912	1625	2687
11	2	2b	2.5	a	2	penult	2	251	102	812	1562	3062
12	2	2b	2.1	a	2	penult	2	207	90	750	1625	3520
1	1	3	4.5	i	2	penult	1	134	70			
2	1	3	6.4	i	2	penult	1	138	86			
3	1	3	4.3	i	2	penult	1	143	92			
4	1	3	5.0	i	2	penult	1	139	110			
5	1	3	3.0	i	2	penult	1	141	90			
6	1	3	4.6	i	2	penult	1	150	84			
7	1	3	8.9	i	2	penult	1	200	67			
8	1	3	14.0	i	2	penult	1	207	74			
9	1	3	12.0	i	2	penult	1	199	42			
10	1	3	6.2	i	2	penult	1	228	88			
11	1	3	4.7	i	2	penult	1	195	72			
12	1	3	2.2	i	2	final	2	202	80			

sub	sex	tok	amp	vow	tone	syl	str	freq	vdur
1	1	3	3.9	i	2	final	2	133	70
2	1	3	4.8	i	2	final	2	133	102
3	1	3	2.7	i	2	final	2	131	106
4	1	3	3.6	i	2	final	2	141	136
5	1	3	2.0	i	2	final	2	139	114
6	1	3	3.0	i	2	final	2	148	89
7	2	3	4.3	i	2	final	2	206	120
8	2	3	8.3	i	2	final	2	213	94
9	2	3	6.9	i	2	final	2	200	77
10	2	3	3.1	i	2	final	2	230	128
11	2	3	4.1	i	2	final	2	200	87
12	2	3	1.4	i	2	final	2	210	88
1	1	3a	2.6	i	2	penult	1	143	58
2	1	3a	9.0	i	2	penult	1	136	80
3	1	3a	4.9	i	2	penult	1	155	60
4	1	3a	10.0	i	2	penult	1	134	53
5	1	3a	5.0	i	2	penult	1	153	78
6	1	3a	5.2	i	2	penult	1	235	62
7	2	3a	1.4	i	2	penult	1	210	77
8	2	3a	7.2	i	2	penult	1	244	80
9	2	3a	12.0	i	2	penult	1	200	76
10	2	3a	5.2	i	2	penult	1	238	82
11	2	3a	7.4	i	2	penult	1	197	90
12	2	3a	4.0	i	2	penult	1	203	120
1	1	3a	.50	i	2	final	2	135	80
2	1	3a	2.0	i	2	final	2	122	100
3	1	3a	1.9	i	2	final	2	141	78

sub	sex	tok	amp	vow	tone	syl	str	freq	vdur	for1	for2	for3
4	1	3a	6.0	i	2	final	2	126	84			
5	1	3a	2.3	i	2	final	2	149	88			
6	1	3a	3.2	i	2	final	2	149	80			
7	2	3a	1.2	i	2	final	2	210	104			
8	2	3a	6.8	i	2	final	2	248	96			
9	2	3a	4.2	i	2	final	2	209	92			
10	2	3a	4.2	i	2	final	2	243	116			
11	2	3a	4.0	i	2	final	2	199	120			
12	2	3a	2.4	i	2	final	2	206	150			
1	1	3b	2.1	i	2	penult	1	143	86	312	2375	3000
2	1	3b	2.5	i	2	penult	1	118	90	312	2125	3000
3	1	3b	8.0	i	2	penult	1	154	76	375	2250	3062
4	1	3b	7.3	i	2	penult	1	120	84	312	2437	3125
5	1	3b	10.0	i	2	penult	1	163	88	375	2375	2875
6	1	3b	2.1	i	2	penult	1	134	76	375	2250	2875
7	2	3b	1.8	i	2	penult	1	227	66	375	2625	3187
8	2	3b	1.7	i	2	penult	1	226	86	312	2625	3187
9	2	3b	9.2	i	2	penult	1	199	74	375	2687	3125
10	2	3b	3.7	i	2	penult	1	227	92	312	2562	2812
11	2	3b	1.7	i	2	penult	1	238	96	375	2687	3178
12	2	3b	3.0	i	2	penult	1	202	76	312	2625	3000
1	1	3b	1.2	i	2	final	2	139	99	312	2375	3000
2	1	3b	1.7	i	2	final	2	112	122	312	2125	3000
3	1	3b	3.2	i	2	final	2	148	100	375	2375	2937
4	1	3b	4.3	i	2	final	2	117	118	312	2437	3125
5	1	3b	6.1	i	2	final	2	153	110	375	2500	3000
6	2	3b	1.3	i	2	final	2	138	80	312	2437	3000

sub	sex	tok	amp	vow	tone	syl	str	freq	vdur	for1	for2	for3
7	2	3b	1.0	i	2	final	2	230	93	437	2625	3187
8	2	3b	1.1	i	2	final	2	230	106	312	2625	3250
9	2	3b	3.0	i	2	final	2	206	90	375	2687	3125
10	2	3b	2.5	i	2	final	2	229	114	312	2812	3187
11	2	3b	1.1	i	2	final	2	243	110	375	2875	3312
12	2	3b	2.2	i	2	final	2	203	84	312	2625	3125
1	1	4	4.1	i	2	final	1	164	72			
2	1	4	7.4	i	2	final	1	137	106			
3	1	4	1.4	i	2	final	1	142	120			
4	1	4	14.1	i	2	final	1	119	114			
5	1	4	8.1	i	2	final	1	147	94			
6	1	4	7.1	i	2	final	1	137	84			
7	2	4	7.9	i	2	final	1	232	107			
8	2	4	7.9	i	2	final	1	243	70			
9	2	4	2.4	i	2	final	1	240	79			
10	2	4	2.4	i	2	final	1	213	98			
11	2	4	1.4	i	2	final	1	227	112			
12	2	4	8.7	i	2	final	1	197	117			
1	1	4	2.0	o	2	penult	2	165	66			
2	1	4	4.9	o	2	penult	2	135	86			
3	1	4	1.1	o	2	penult	2	140	100			
4	1	4	6.1	o	2	penult	2	118	75			
5	1	4	3.7	o	2	penult	2	143	70			
6	1	4	4.7	o	2	penult	2	135	63			
7	2	4	4.5	o	2	penult	2	230	87			
8	2	4	4.5	o	2	penult	2	240	72			
9	2	4	1.6	o	2	penult	2	244	66			

sub	sex	tok	amp	vow	tone	syl	str	freq	vdur
10	2	4	.24	o	2	penult	2	203	86
11	2	4	1.3	o	2	penult	2	232	104
12	2	4	6.4	o	2	penult	2	194	89
1	1	4a	8.1	i	2	final	1	165	142
2	1	4a	8.6	i	2	final	1	123	94
3	1	4a	3.6	i	2	final	1	173	74
4	1	4a	1.9	i	2	final	1	131	113
5	1	4a	1.7	i	2	final	1	160	70
6	1	4a	9.3	i	2	final	1	144	94
7	2	4a	2.1	i	2	final	1	263	78
8	2	4a	4.5	i	2	final	1	233	77
9	2	4a	18.0	i	2	final	1	253	73
10	2	4a	4.2	i	2	final	1	247	92
11	2	4a	3.0	i	2	final	1	215	180
12	2	4a	4.6	i	2	final	1	251	117
1	1	4a	6.4	o	2	penult	2	166	90
2	1	4a	4.2	o	2	penult	2	129	80
3	1	4a	2.7	o	2	penult	2	169	62
4	1	4a	1.6	o	2	penult	2	128	92
5	1	4a	.8	o	2	penult	2	160	50
6	1	4a	1.1	o	2	penult	2	142	70
7	2	4a	1.1	o	2	penult	2	260	62
8	2	4a	3.2	o	2	penult	2	238	71
9	2	4a	4.2	o	2	penult	2	253	54
10	2	4a	1.5	o	2	penult	2	233	66
11	2	4a	1.0	o	2	penult	2	216	116
12	2	4a	1.8	o	2	penult	2	187	98

sub	sex	tok	amp	vow	tone	syl	str	freq	vdur	for1	for2	for3
1	1	4b	17.0	i	2	final	1	170	134			
2	1	4b	6.2	i	2	final	1	136	82			
3	1	4b	2.5	i	2	final	1	160	96			
4	1	4b	1.7	i	2	final	1	120	70			
5	1	4b	3.8	i	2	final	1	160	70			
6	1	4b	2.2	i	2	final	1	176	82			
7	2	4b	11.0	i	2	final	1	234	87			
8	2	4b	3.7	i	2	final	1	217	102			
9	2	4b	13.0	i	2	final	1	240	83			
10	2	4b	2.2	i	2	final	1	265	65			
11	2	4b	2.2	i	2	final	1	215	180			
12	2	4b	2.3	i	2	final	1	205	83			
1	1	4b	8	o	2	penult	2	166	97			
2	1	4b	4.9	o	2	penult	2	130	76			
3	1	4b	1.9	o	2	penult	2	158	67			
4	1	4b	1.1	o	2	penult	2	120	70			
5	1	4b	1.2	o	2	penult	2	150	50			
6	1	4b	1.5	o	2	penult	2	167	62			
7	2	4b	1.2	o	2	penult	2	224	55			
8	2	4b	2.3	o	2	penult	2	222	98			
9	2	4b	3.4	o	2	penult	2	240	60			
10	2	4b	1.3	o	2	penult	2	265	65			
11	2	4b	1.6	o	2	penult	2	259	106			
12	2	4b	1.9	o	2	penult	2	200	50			
1	1	5	3.3	i	1	penult	1	170	46	437	2125	2815
2	1	5	2.5	i	1	penult	1	180	51	437	1937	2500
3	1	5	5.4	i	1	penult	1	173	72	437	2062	2875

sub	sex	tok	amp	vow	tone	syl	str	freq	vdur	for1	for2	for3
4	1	5	6.7	i	1	penult	1	162	81	375	2250	3500
5	1	5	4.7	i	1	penult	1	163	54	437	2187	2875
6	1	5	5.9	i	1	penult	1	177	44	375	2250	2750
7	2	5	7.4	i	1	penult	1	348	51	500	2687	3375
8	2	5	4.3	i	1	penult	1	252	73	500	2500	3000
9	2	5	5.1	i	1	penult	1	277	52	437	2625	3375
10	2	5	2.4	i	1	penult	1	240	92	500	2312	2937
11	2	5	1.4	i	1	penult	1	305	72	500	2437	3125
12	2	5	3.2	i	1	penult	1	253	90	500	2437	3000
1	1	5	2.3	i	1	final	2	180	64	437	2125	2812
2	1	5	1.8	i	1	final	2	176	81	437	1937	3000
3	1	5	3.5	i	1	final	2	180	86	437	2312	3000
4	1	5	4.0	i	1	final	2	160	95	375	2375	3625
5	1	5	3.7	i	1	final	2	169	88	437	2187	2750
6	1	5	2.3	i	1	final	2	170	67	375	2375	2750
7	2	5	3.3	i	1	final	2	347	88	500	2687	3375
8	2	5	2.9	i	1	final	2	250	85	500	2500	3000
9	2	5	3.2	i	1	final	2	277	68	437	2635	337
10	2	5	2.0	i	1	final	2	238	126	500	2312	2937
11	2	5	1.1	i	1	final	2	308	93	500	2437	3125
12	2	5	2.6	i	1	final	2	249	121	500	2437	3000
1	1	5a	6.4	i	1	penult	1	154				
2	1	5a	1.3	i	1	penult	1	177				
3	1	5a	9.8	i	1	penult	1	155				
4	1	5a	5.6	i	1	penult	1	159				
5	1	5a	3.2	i	1	penult	1	167				
6	1	5a	5.4	i	1	penult	1	151				

sub	sex	tok	amp	vow	tone	syl	str	freq
7	2	5a	2.6	i	1	penult	1	336
8	2	5a	4.7	i	1	penult	1	286
9	2	5a	5.7	i	1	penult	1	296
10	2	5a	2.1	i	1	penult	1	295
11	2	5a	4.2	i	1	penult	1	297
12	2	5a	4.8	i	1	penult	1	270
1	1	5a	5.2	i	1	final	2	155
2	1	5a	1.0	i	1	final	2	181
3	1	5a	6.7	i	1	final	2	157
4	1	5a	4.0	i	1	final	2	158
5	1	5a	2.2	i	1	final	2	170
6	1	5a	3.8	i	1	final	2	153
7	2	5a	1.4	i	1	final	2	325
8	2	5a	3.7	i	1	final	2	300
9	2	5a	4.6	i	1	final	2	294
10	2	5a	1.5	i	1	final	2	285
11	2	5a	3.8	i	1	final	2	308
12	2	5a	4.4	i	1	final	2	280
1	1	5b	4.0	i	1	penult	1	163
2	1	5b	2.0	i	1	penult	1	200
3	1	5b	1.8	i	1	penult	1	179
4	1	5b	5.5	i	1	penult	1	160
5	1	5b	3.6	i	1	penult	1	171
6	1	5b	1.4	i	1	penult	1	150
7	2	5b	3.3	i	1	penult	1	324
8	2	5b	4.7	i	1	penult	1	313
9	2	5b	5.7	i	1	penult	1	277

sub	sex	tok	amp	vow	tone	syl	str	freq	vdur	for1	for2	for3
10	2	5b	2.4	i	1	penult	1	294				
12	2	5b	4.5	i	1	penult	1	253				
1	1	5b	2.7	i	1	final	2	158				
2	1	5b	1.7	i	1	final	2	200				
3	1	5b	.9	i	1	final	2	177				
4	1	5b	2.8	i	1	final	2	160				
5	1	5b	3.0	i	1	final	2	160				
6	1	5b	1.1	i	1	final	2	145				
7	2	5b	1.6	i	1	final	2	306				
8	2	5b	3.7	i	1	final	2	306				
9	2	5b	4.3	i	1	final	2	276				
10	2	5b	1.4	i	1	final	2	285				
12	2	5b	4.2	i	1	final	2	247				
1	1	6	7.2	oo	2	final	1	169		500	937	2375
2	1	6	1.7	oo	2	final	1	194		500	875	2375
3	1	6	12.1	oo	2	final	1	167		500	1000	2562
4	1	6	7.4	oo	2	final	1	166		500	1125	2500
5	1	6	9.2	oo	2	final	1	170		562	1000	2250
6	1	6	3.6	oo	2	final	1	170		437	1125	2625
7	2	6	3.5	oo	2	final	1	289		500	1125	2625
8	2	6	10.0	oo	2	final	1	269		500	1000	3250
9	2	6	3.8	oo	2	final	1	285		500	875	2875
10	2	6	3.5	oo	2	final	1	274		500	1125	3062
11	2	6	1.2	oo	2	final	1	250		500	1125	2937
12	2	6	5.1	oo	2	final	1	239		437	1125	3000
1	1	6	3.4	oo	2	penult	2	172		500	1125	2750
2	1	6	1.0	oo	2	penult	2	187		500	1187	2687

sub	sex	tok	amp	vow	tone	syl	str	freq	vdur	for1	for2	for3
3	1	6	8.6	oo	2	penult	2	163		500	1000	2562
4	1	6	6.7	oo	2	penult	2	165		500	1125	2500
5	1	6	8.1	oo	2	penult	2	165		562	1125	2562
6	1	6	2.9	oo	2	penult	2	169		437	1125	2625
7	2	6	2.8	oo	2	penult	2	286		500	1125	3125
8	2	6	6.1	oo	2	penult	2	266		500	1000	3250
9	2	6	2.2	oo	2	penult	2	275		500	1250	3000
10	2	6	2.6	oo	2	penult	2	260		500	1437	3187
11	2	6	1.2	oo	2	penult	2	250		500	1125	2937
12	2	6	3.6	oo	2	penult	2	232		500	1125	3000
1	1	7	3.6	i	2	penult	1	163	72	500	1875	2625
2	1	7	2.7	i	2	penult	1	125	76	437	2500	3062
3	1	7	3.8	i	2	penult	1	153	80	500	2312	3187
4	1	7	5.9	i	2	penult	1	125	78	375	2437	3125
5	1	7	6.1	i	2	penult	1	160	74	500	2312	2937
6	1	7	3.8	i	2	penult	1	163	73	437	1937	2625
7	2	7	5.9	i	2	penult	1	253	66	437	2437	3062
8	2	7	4.3	i	2	penult	1	250	60	437	3062	3500
9	2	7	6.1	i	2	penult	1	208	84	375	2625	3187
10	2	7	2.5	i	2	penult	1	240	65	500	2625	3125
11	2	7	2.5	i	2	penult	1	240	53	437	2437	3187
12	2	7	2.6	i	2	penult	1	215	97	375	2625	3187
1	1	7	3.1	i	2	final	2	167	116	500	1875	2625
2	1	7	2.3	i	2	final	2	126	106	437	2500	3062
3	1	7	3.2	i	2	final	2	154	104	500	2312	3187
4	1	7	3.4	i	2	final	2	117	104	375	2437	3125
5	1	7	4.3	i	2	final	2	156	116	500	2312	2937

sub	sex	tok	amp	vow	tone	syl	str	freq	vdur	for1	for2	for3
6	1	7	3.1	i	2	final	2	168	115	437	1937	2625
7	2	7	3.8	i	2	final	2	252	80	437	2437	3062
8	2	7	2.8	i	2	final	2	250	88	437	3062	3500
9	2	7	4.7	i	2	final	2	208	104	375	2625	3187
10	2	7	2.1	i	2	final	2	238	118	500	2625	3125
11	2	7	1.0	i	2	final	2	239	96	437	2437	3187
12	2	7	2.0	i	2	final	2	216	118	375	2625	3187
1	1	7a	4.8	i	2	penult	1	152				
2	1	7a	3.1	i	2	penult	1	114				
3	1	7a	3.0	i	2	penult	1	144				
4	1	7a	3.2	i	2	penult	1	120				
5	1	7a	6.0	i	2	penult	1	159				
6	1	7a	7.5	i	2	penult	1	137				
7	2	7a	2.2	i	2	penult	1	240				
8	2	7a	1.9	i	2	penult	1	250				
9	2	7a	1.5	i	2	penult	1	256				
10	2	7a	2.7	i	2	penult	1	219				
11	2	7a	3.7	i	2	penult	1	208				
12	2	7a	1.8	i	2	penult	1	195				
1	1	7a	4.9	i	2	final	2	130				
2	1	7a	2.2	i	2	final	2	107				
3	1	7a	2.1	i	2	final	2	145				
4	1	7a	2.1	i	2	final	2	127				
5	1	7a	4.2	i	2	final	2	155				
6	1	7a	5.2	i	2	final	2	142				
7	2	7a	1.9	i	2	final	2	239				
8	2	7a	.9	i	2	final	2	253				

sub	sex	tok	amp	vow	tone	syl	str	freq
9	2	7a	.8	i	2	final	2	252
10	2	7a	2.0	i	2	final	2	210
11	2	7a	2.7	i	2	final	2	200
12	2	7a	2.4	i	2	final	2	199
1	1	7b	10.0	i	2	penult	1	139
2	1	7b	2.7	i	2	penult	1	112
3	1	7b	8.6	i	2	penult	1	138
4	1	7b	2.7	i	2	penult	1	123
5	1	7b	3.3	i	2	penult	1	150
6	1	7b	2.6	i	2	penult	1	137
7	2	7b	5.0	i	2	penult	1	242
8	2	7b	3.6	i	2	penult	1	228
10	2	7b	8.7	i	2	penult	1	251
11	2	7b	2.2	i	2	penult	1	202
12	2	7b	2.9	i	2	penult	1	197
1	1	7b	1.0	i	2	final	2	149
2	1	7b	2.3	i	2	final	2	110
3	1	7b	7.9	i	2	final	2	132
4	1	7b	1.7	i	2	final	2	112
5	1	7b	2.4	i	2	final	2	142
6	1	7b	2.2	i	2	final	2	141
7	2	7b	3.8	i	2	final	2	242
8	2	7b	2.1	i	2	final	2	229
10	2	7b	5.9	i	2	final	2	249
11	2	7b	1.6	i	2	final	2	192
12	2	7b	1.3	i	2	final	2	195
1	1	8	3.1	a	2	penult	1	132

sub	sex	tok	amp	vow	tone	syl	str	freq	vdur
2	1	8	5.4	a	2	penult	1	116	
3	1	8	1.8	a	2	penult	1	124	
4	1	8	12.0	a	2	penult	1	116	
5	1	8	3.4	a	2	penult	1	131	
6	1	8	1.8	a	2	penult	1	118	
7	2	8	10.0	a	2	penult	1	203	
8	2	8	7.0	a	2	penult	1	213	
9	2	8	3.4	a	2	penult	1	182	
10	2	8	3.1	a	2	penult	1	189	
11	2	8	1.9	a	2	penult	1	189	
12	2	8	2.2	a	2	penult	1	181	
1	1	8	2.3	i	1	final	2	172	
2	1	8	.78	i	1	final	2	146	
3	1	8	.90	i	1	final	2	152	
4	1	8	2.1	i	1	final	2	161	
5	1	8	2.9	i	1	final	2	175	
6	1	8	.71	i	1	final	2	145	
7	2	8	4.6	i	1	final	2	301	
8	2	8	5.0	i	1	final	2	333	
9	2	8	.69	i	1	final	2	242	
10	2	8	1.6	i	1	final	2	282	
11	2	8	1.3	i	1	final	2	282	
12	2	8	1.4	i	1	final	2	250	
1	1	9	3.2	i	1	final	1	209	124
2	1	9	3.3	i	1	final	1	161	70
3	1	9	3.6	i	1	final	1	205	90
4	1	9	2.2	i	1	final	1	155	102

sub	sex	tok	amp	vow	tone	syl	str	freq	vdur
5	1	9	6.4	i	1	final	1	260	68
6	1	9	2.6	i	1	final	1	174	116
7	2	9	1.8	i	1	final	1	327	90
8	2	9	4.7	i	1	final	1	369	94
9	2	9	1.8	i	1	final	1	310	130
10	2	9	2.4	i	1	final	1	327	65
11	2	9	2.4	i	1	final	1	325	170
12	2	9	6.7	i	1	final	1	258	124
1	1	9	2.2	i	2	penult	2	160	94
2	1	9	1.7	i	2	penult	2	124	52
3	1	9	2.8	i	2	penult	2	167	74
4	1	9	.65	i	2	penult	2	123	82
5	1	9	3.6	i	2	penult	2	182	42
6	1	9	1.9	i	2	penult	2	145	94
7	2	9	1.3	i	2	penult	2	288	64
8	2	9	2.0	i	2	penult	2	262	60
9	2	9	1.4	i	2	penult	2	259	102
10	2	9	1.0	i	2	penult	2	243	40
11	2	9	.80	i	2	penult	2	225	92
12	2	9	4.4	i	2	penult	2	198	96
1	1	10	8.8	a	2	final	1	162	
2	1	10	3.4	a	2	final	1	123	
3	1	10	2.2	a	2	final	1	184	
4	1	10	4.2	a	2	final	1	136	
5	1	10	1.7	a	2	final	1	197	
6	1	10	7.0	a	2	final	1	132	
7	2	10	5.7	a	2	final	1	269	

sub	sex	tok	amp	vow	tone	syl	str	freq
8	2	10	5.7	a	2	final	1	258
9	2	10	1.8	a	2	final	1	253
10	2	10	1.3	a	2	final	1	240
11	2	10	2.8	a	2	final	1	195
12	2	10	5.6	a	2	final	1	240
1	1	10	2.1	i	1	penult	2	192
2	1	10	2.6	i	1	penult	2	145
3	1	10	.20	i	1	penult	2	209
4	1	10	2.0	i	1	penult	2	155
5	1	10	.15	i	1	penult	2	260
6	1	10	.21	i	1	penult	2	152
7	2	10	2.0	i	1	penult	2	333
8	2	10	3.9	i	1	penult	2	307
9	2	10	.50	i	1	penult	2	300
10	2	10	.51	i	1	penult	2	286
11	2	10	1.4	i	1	penult	2	242
12	2	10	3.2	i	1	penult	2	200
1	1	11	9.7	aa	1	antip	1	175
2	1	11	4.9	aa	1	antip	1	174
3	1	11	5.8	aa	1	antip	1	185
4	1	11	4.1	aa	1	antip	1	137
5	1	11	5.8	aa	1	antip	1	185
6	1	11	3.3	aa	1	antip	1	138
7	2	11	2.3	aa	1	antip	1	241
8	2	11	1.5	aa	1	antip	1	240
9	2	11	1.2	aa	1	antip	1	229
10	2	11	1.4	aa	1	antip	1	255

sub	sex	tok	amp	vow	tone	syl	str	freq
11	2	11	1.8	aa	1	antip	1	243
12	2	11	9.6	aa	1	antip	1	230
1	1	11	1.7	i	1	penult	2	179
2	1	11	1.7	i	1	penult	2	181
3	1	11	.50	i	1	penult	2	189
4	1	11	.14	i	1	penult	2	134
5	1	11	.58	i	1	penult	2	181
6	1	11	1.0	i	1	penult	2	146
7	2	11	1.9	i	1	penult	2	248
8	2	11	.30	i	1	penult	2	232
9	2	11	.30	i	1	penult	2	238
10	2	11	.40	i	1	penult	2	258
11	2	11	1.5	i	1	penult	2	248
12	2	11	1.4	i	1	penult	2	249
1	1	12	9.7	aa	1	antip	1	175
2	1	12	4.9	aa	1	antip	1	125
3	1	12	5.8	aa	1	antip	1	185
4	1	12	4.1	aa	1	antip	1	135
5	1	12	5.8	aa	1	antip	1	185
6	1	12	3.3	aa	1	antip	1	138
7	2	12	2.3	aa	1	antip	1	241
8	2	12	1.5	aa	1	antip	1	240
9	2	12	1.2	aa	1	antip	1	229
10	2	12	1.4	aa	1	antip	1	255
11	2	12	1.8	aa	1	antip	1	243
12	2	12	9.6	aa	1	antip	1	230
1	1	12	.7	i	1	final	2	176

sub	sex	tok	amp	vow	tone	syl	str	freq
2	1	12	1.2	i	1	final	2	133
3	1	12	.40	i	1	final	2	180
4	1	12	.10	i	1	final	2	131
5	1	12	.41	i	1	final	2	192
6	1	12	.50	i	1	final	2	134
7	2	12	1.5	i	1	final	2	237
8	2	12	.30	i	1	final	2	248
9	2	12	.30	i	1	final	2	234
10	2	12	.20	i	1	final	2	259
11	2	12	1.3	i	1	final	2	243
12	2	12	1.4	i	1	final	2	249
1	1	13	10.0	i	2	final	1	133
2	1	13	1.4	i	2	final	1	115
3	1	13	4.2	i	2	final	1	120
4	1	13	2.0	i	2	final	1	125
5	1	13	10.0	i	2	final	1	130
6	1	13	6.7	i	2	final	1	133
7	2	13	2.6	i	2	final	1	239
8	2	13	3.2	i	2	final	1	241
9	2	13	3.4	i	2	final	1	241
10	2	13	2.4	i	2	final	1	240
11	2	13	12.1	i	2	final	1	228
12	2	13	9.1	i	2	final	1	143
1	1	13	1.6	i	1	penult	2	153
2	1	13	1.1	i	1	penult	2	135
3	1	13	3.7	i	1	penult	2	158
4	1	13	1.6	i	1	penult	2	156

sub	sex	tok	amp	vow	tone	syl	str	freq
5	1	13	4.1	i	1	penult	2	151
6	1	13	1.0	i	1	penult	2	159
7	2	13	1.7	i	1	penult	2	311
8	2	13	1.5	i	1	penult	2	280
9	2	13	1.5	i	1	penult	2	280
10	2	13	1.6	i	1	penult	2	311
11	2	13	9.2	i	1	penult	2	291
12	2	13	6.1	i	1	penult	2	237
1	1	14	13.0	ai	2	final	1	154
2	1	14	4.4	ai	2	final	1	125
3	1	14	12.0	ai	2	final	1	131
4	1	14	6.8	ai	2	final	1	131
5	1	14	2.5	ai	2	final	1	189
6	1	14	8.6	ai	2	final	1	160
7	2	14	13.0	ai	2	final	1	275
8	2	14	3.0	ai	2	final	1	221
9	2	14	13.0	ai	2	final	1	225
10	2	14	15.0	ai	2	final	1	237
11	2	14	2.4	ai	2	final	1	210
12	2	14	4.0	ai	2	final	1	215
1	1	14	8.0	o	2	penult	2	146
2	1	14	2.8	o	2	penult	2	130
3	1	14	6.3	o	2	penult	2	131
4	1	14	3.4	o	2	penult	2	125
5	1	14	1.2	o	2	penult	2	195
6	1	14	5.8	o	2	penult	2	160
7	2	14	6.5	o	2	penult	2	279

sub	sex	tok	amp	vow	tone	syl	str	freq
8	2	14	2.5	o	2	penult	2	230
9	2	14	8.7	o	2	penult	2	239
10	2	14	12.0	o	2	penult	2	250
11	2	14	2.0	o	2	penult	2	209
12	2	14	2.4	o	2	penult	2	217
1	1	15	3.2	a	2	final	1	139
2	1	15	4.0	a	2	final	1	109
3	1	15	3.5	a	2	final	1	130
4	1	15	11.0	a	2	final	1	120
5	1	15	12.0	a	2	final	1	140
6	1	15	12.0	a	2	final	1	135
7	2	15	8.3	a	2	final	1	240
8	2	15	6.8	a	2	final	1	224
9	2	15	12.1	a	2	final	1	190
10	2	15	5.3	a	2	final	1	217
11	2	15	6.1	a	2	final	1	232
12	2	15	15.0	a	2	final	1	196
1	1	15	1.4	a	2	antip	2	134
2	1	15	1.7	a	2	antip	2	110
3	1	15	1.5	a	2	antip	2	138
4	1	15	3.7	a	2	antip	2	107
5	1	15	5.5	a	2	antip	2	157
6	1	15	5.6	a	2	antip	2	133
7	2	15	3.7	a	2	antip	2	237
8	2	15	3.8	a	2	antip	2	216
9	2	15	5.4	a	2	antip	2	177
10	2	15	3.5	a	2	antip	2	202

sub	sex	tok	amp	vow	tone	syl	str	freq	vdur
11	2	15	2.5	a	2	antip	2	228	
12	2	15	5.6	a	2	antip	2	197	
1	1	16	3.2	a	2	final	1	139	60
2	1	16	4.0	a	2	final	1	109	104
3	1	16	3.5	a	2	final	1	130	108
4	1	16	11.0	a	2	final	1	120	98
5	1	16	12.0	a	2	final	1	140	98
6	1	16	12.0	a	2	final	1	135	74
7	2	16	8.3	a	2	final	1	240	79
8	2	16	6.8	a	2	final	1	224	76
9	2	16	12.1	a	2	final	1	190	69
10	2	16	5.3	a	2	final	1	217	74
11	2	16	6.1	a	2	final	1	232	78
12	2	16	15.0	a	2	final	1	196	64
1	1	16	2.8	a	2	penult	2	133	42
2	1	16	2.1	a	2	penult	2	109	80
3	1	16	2.8	a	2	penult	2	136	72
4	1	16	6.8	a	2	penult	2	121	88
5	1	16	8.8	a	2	penult	2	142	76
6	1	16	8.0	a	2	penult	2	137	56
7	2	16	4.4	a	2	penult	2	236	57
8	2	16	5.2	a	2	penult	2	220	30
9	2	16	6.6	a	2	penult	2	185	73
10	2	16	1.9	a	2	penult	2	223	60
11	2	16	2.5	a	2	penult	2	224	61
12	2	16	9.6	a	2	penult	2	197	60
1	1	17	5.0	ii	2	antip	1	148	

sub	sex	tok	amp	vow	tone	syl	str	freq
2	1	17	2.9	ii	2	antip	1	116
3	1	17	7.9	ii	2	antip	1	146
4	1	17	3.8	ii	2	antip	1	105
5	1	17	2.2	ii	2	antip	1	170
6	1	17	15.4	ii	2	antip	1	170
7	2	17	15.0	ii	2	antip	1	275
8	2	17	5.0	ii	2	antip	1	205
9	2	17	7.6	ii	2	antip	1	255
10	2	17	4.0	ii	2	antip	1	232
11	2	17	2.9	ii	2	antip	1	224
12	2	17	3.3	ii	2	antip	1	223
1	1	17	2.8	i	2	penult	2	152
2	1	17	1.7	i	2	penult	2	117
3	1	17	2.6	i	2	penult	2	144
4	1	17	1.7	i	2	penult	2	104
5	1	17	1.1	i	2	penult	2	161
6	1	17	1.2	i	2	penult	2	167
7	2	17	6.8	i	2	penult	2	283
8	2	17	2.2	i	2	penult	2	205
9	2	17	5.0	i	2	penult	2	262
10	2	17	2.0	i	2	penult	2	235
11	2	17	1.8	i	2	penult	2	235
12	2	17	2.1	i	2	penult	2	227
1	1	18	5.0	ii	2	antip	1	148
2	1	18	2.9	ii	2	antip	1	116
3	1	18	7.9	ii	2	antip	1	146
4	1	18	3.8	ii	2	antip	1	105

sub	sex	tok	amp	vow	tone	syl	str	freq	vdur	for1	for2	for3
5	1	18	2.2	ii	2	antip	1	170				
6	1	18	15.4	ii	2	antip	1	170				
7	2	18	15.0	ii	2	antip	1	275				
8	2	18	5.0	ii	2	antip	1	205				
9	2	18	7.6	ii	2	antip	1	255				
10	2	18	4.0	ii	2	antip	1	232				
11	2	18	2.9	ii	2	antip	1	224				
12	2	18	3.3	ii	2	antip	1	223				
1	1	18	1.5	i	2	final	2	145				
2	1	18	1.4	i	2	final	2	124				
3	1	18	4.0	i	2	final	2	145				
4	1	18	2.2	i	2	final	2	113				
5	1	18	.40	i	2	final	2	175				
6	1	18	1.0	i	2	final	2	173				
7	2	18	6.3	i	2	final	2	295				
8	2	18	2.5	i	2	final	2	213				
9	2	18	5.0	i	2	final	2	276				
10	2	18	1.0	i	2	final	2	241				
11	2	18	1.6	i	2	final	2	236				
12	2	18	1.9	i	2	final	2	232				

Section 2: Duration of intervocalic consonants /b/ and /g/ in stressed and unstressed positions

Interpretation of columns:

tok(*en*): words used for measuring intervocalic consonant length
1=kà'bà 'not'
1a=first repetition
1b=second repetition
2=gàbà' 'Jacamar'
2a=first repetition

2b=second repetition
3=pì'gì 'swift'
3a=first repetition
3b=second repetition
4=bògì' 'chest'
4a=first repetition
4b=second repetition

sub(ject): speaker number
sex: 1=male; 2=female
con(sonant): /b/; /g/
cdur: consonant duration; measurements in milliseconds
str(ess): 1=stressed 2=unstressed

sub	sex	tok	con	cdur	str
1	1	1	b	32	2
2	1	1	b	34	2
3	1	1	b	55	2
4	1	1	b	30	2
5	1	1	b	34	2
6	1	1	b	36	2
7	2	1	b	68	2
8	2	1	b	52	2
9	2	1	b	48	2
10	2	1	b	47	2
11	2	1	b	36	2
12	2	1	b	60	2
1	1	1a	b	38	2
2	1	1a	b	55	2
3	1	1a	b	34	2
4	1	1a	b	25	2
5	1	1a	b	35	2

sub	sex	tok	con	cdur	str
6	1	1a	b	30	2
7	2	1a	b	43	2
8	2	1a	b	58	2
9	2	1a	b	41	2
10	2	1a	b	28	2
11	2	1a	b	44	2
12	2	1a	b	44	2
1	1	1b	b	36	2
2	1	1b	b	40	2
3	1	1b	b	20	2
4	1	1b	b	30	2
5	1	1b	b	20	2
6	2	1b	b	58	2
7	2	1b	b	38	2
8	2	1b	b	34	2
9	2	1b	b	23	2
10	2	1b	b	52	2
11	2	1b	b	29	2
12	2	1b	b	32	2
1	1	2	b	60	1
2	1	2	b	64	1
3	1	2	b	61	1
4	1	2	b	48	1
5	1	2	b	48	1
6	1	2	b	62	1
7	2	2	b	50	1
8	2	2	b	62	1

sub	sex	tok	con	cdur	str
9	2	2	b	58	1
10	2	2	b	48	1
11	2	2	b	70	1
12	2	2	b	76	1
1	1	2a	b	60	1
2	1	2a	b	62	1
3	1	2a	b	56	1
4	1	2a	b	60	1
5	1	2a	b	50	1
6	1	2a	b	70	1
7	2	2a	b	62	1
8	2	2a	b	54	1
9	2	2a	b	88	1
10	2	2a	b	60	1
11	2	2a	b	66	1
12	2	2a	b	74	1
1	1	2b	b	68	1
2	1	2b	b	66	1
3	1	2b	b	87	1
5	1	2b	b	58	1
6	1	2b	b	84	1
7	1	2b	b	60	1
8	2	2b	b	82	1
9	2	2b	b	84	1
10	2	2b	b	60	1
11	2	2b	b	68	1
12	2	2b	b	86	1

sub	sex	tok	con	cdur	str
1	1	3	g	54	2
2	1	3	g	57	2
3	1	3	g	44	2
4	1	3	g	64	2
5	1	3	g	52	2
6	1	3	g	52	2
7	2	3	g	46	2
8	2	3	g	50	2
9	2	3	g	42	2
10	2	3	g	80	2
11	2	3	g	50	2
12	2	3	g	48	2
1	1	3a	g	46	2
2	1	3a	g	42	2
3	1	3a	g	56	2
4	1	3a	g	48	2
5	1	3a	g	38	2
6	1	3a	g	49	2
7	2	3a	g	45	2
8	2	3a	g	34	2
9	2	3a	g	50	2
10	2	3a	g	40	2
11	2	3a	g	54	2
12	2	3a	g	60	2
1	1	3b	g	34	2
2	1	3b	g	48	2
3	1	3b	g	40	2

sub	sex	tok	con	cdur	str
4	1	3b	g	42	2
5	1	3b	g	39	2
6	1	3b	g	38	2
7	2	3b	g	50	2
8	2	3b	g	46	2
9	2	3b	g	42	2
10	2	3b	g	42	2
11	2	3b	g	56	2
12	2	3b	g	60	2
1	1	4	g	87	1
2	1	4	g	68	1
3	1	4	g	55	1
4	1	4	g	66	1
5	1	4	g	52	1
6	1	4	g	66	1
7	2	4	g	80	1
8	2	4	g	86	1
9	2	4	g	90	1
10	2	4	g	83	1
11	2	4	g	78	1
12	2	4	g	117	1
1	1	4a	g	60	1
2	1	4a	g	70	1
3	1	4a	g	61	1
4	1	4a	g	70	1
5	1	4a	g	58	1
6	1	4a	g	84	1

sub	sex	tok	con	cdur	str
7	2	4a	g	61	1
8	2	4a	g	64	1
9	2	4a	g	73	1
10	2	4a	g	64	1
11	2	4a	g	108	1
12	2	4a	g	128	1
1	1	4b	g	60	1
2	1	4b	g	74	1
3	1	4b	g	68	1
4	1	4b	g	76	1
5	1	4b	g	82	1
6	1	4b	g	72	1
7	2	4b	g	51	1
8	2	4b	g	73	1
9	2	4b	g	70	1
10	2	4b	g	77	1
11	2	4b	g	94	1
12	2	4b	g	113	1